CAMBRIDGE CLASSICAL STUDIES

General Editors: W. K. C. GUTHRIE, A. H. M. JONES, D. L. PAGE

THE
WOODWORK OF
GREEK ROOFS

THE
WOODWORK OF
GREEK ROOFS

BY

A. TREVOR HODGE

CAMBRIDGE
AT THE UNIVERSITY PRESS
1960

CAMBRIDGE UNIVERSITY PRESS
Cambridge, New York, Melbourne, Madrid, Cape Town, Singapore,
São Paulo, Delhi, Dubai, Tokyo

Cambridge University Press
The Edinburgh Building, Cambridge CB2 8RU, UK

Published in the United States of America by Cambridge University Press, New York

www.cambridge.org
Information on this title: www.cambridge.org/9780521141123

First published 1960
This digitally printed version 2010

A catalogue record for this publication is available from the British Library

ISBN 978-0-521-05280-1 Hardback
ISBN 978-0-521-14112-3 Paperback

CONTENTS

v

LIST OF ILLUSTRATIONS

FIGURES

PREFACE

In this book I have not tried to give a comprehensive account of every facet of Greek roofing. There are many areas in which speculation remains our only guide, and these I have avoided, preferring to set out the actual concrete evidence available rather than to discuss points which, however important, must remain conjectural. This is why there is no discussion of early pre-sixth century roofs or the origin of triglyphs, and little of the hypaethral question; I have no new evidence to bring to bear on these matters, and prefer to use my space for the problems where I have. This book, in short, is conceived as a guide to what we know, not what we don't know.

It also ploughs something of a lone furrow, for, with the exception of the attic, no part of the Greek temple has been less studied than the roofing woodwork. The subject has only been touched on desultorily in the general publications, and scholars restoring one particular building have tended to concentrate on the evidence offered by it alone without viewing it in the light of what is known from other sites.

This is chiefly because nowhere do there survive actual remains of the beams, and so it has all too often been assumed that nothing is to be learned from the monuments themselves. Instead, study has been concentrated on the descriptions found in building inscriptions, and from this has crystallized the conception of a standard form of Greek roofing. Accordingly, most reconstructions either adopt this form, often even if the building concerned is quite unsuited to it, or, in an honest confession of ignorance, leave the whole area between the ceiling and the tiles tactfully blank.

There has thus been no attempt to collect and correlate all the evidence available, and form some coherent picture of Greek roofing; and any views that scholars hold on the subject tend to be expressed only in the form of asides tucked away in foot-notes, or odd sentences buried in the body of a text dealing with something quite different. I have therefore found little to help me directly in the published works.

The most fruitful source of evidence I found to be the cuttings in the stonework of the actual buildings. Little was to be learned from a study of the terra-cotta revetments that covered so many of the early Greek buildings in Sicily, and representations of architectural scenes on vases do not seem to be accurate enough to be relied on. House models are generally too early in date to give evidence of any value to our study, except for Etruscan roofing.

Dealing with so many buildings I have been able to devote a close personal study only to those parts directly concerned with the roofing. For the spacing of the walls, siting of the columns, height of the entablature, and similar basic features, I have had to accept without checking the published restorations. Thus in my restorations of the four temples that I have taken as particular examples of Greek roofing in the first part of this study, the size, placing and disposition of the roofing timbers are the result of my own measurements on the site; the general proportions of the buildings reproduce the work of other scholars.

The measurements of the actual timbers are, however, all my own, unless it is expressly stated otherwise. I have visited all buildings offering any evidence bearing on the subject, and all conclusions and detailed measurements are the results of my own observation.

It is both a duty and a pleasure to acknowledge the efforts of those who have assisted me. First must come Dr W. H. Plommer, of Cambridge, who originally suggested roofing to me as a subject that might repay investigation; I have also profited greatly throughout my work from his ready advice and acute criticism, without which this study would indeed be but a sorry thing. Nor can I overlook the claims of Mr R. M. Cook, whose advice often proved of the greatest value.

In Italy I must acknowledge the generous assistance of Mr J. B. Ward Perkins, Director of the British School at Rome. Professor A. Maiuri, Superintendent of Antiquities at Naples, very kindly had drawn for me the section of the Casa del Telaio which I have included as fig. 14, and gave permission to reproduce it in this present work. Professor G. Caputo provided the photograph of the Etruscan chest lid shown in Pl. VIIIc, which is under his care at Florence. To the Superintendent at Salerno, Professor P. C. Sestieri, I am particularly indebted, for he provided not only photographs and details of the underground shrine at Paestum, but also the necessary men and ladders to enable me to get up on top of the temples of Ceres and Poseidon. When the question of ladders arose again at Agrigento, Professor P. Griffo could not have been more co-operative or generous in his assistance.

In Greece I must record my gratitude to the then Director of the British School at Athens, Mr J. M. Cook, both for welcome words of encouragement and valuable hints on technique. I cannot omit my debt to Mr Miliades, the Ephor of the Acropolis, who gave me *carte blanche* to climb about over the buildings in his charge as much and as often as I liked, and to the authorities of the French School for facilitating my work at Delphi. Without the aid of the American staff of the Agora excavations, who once more obliged with ladders and photographs (Pl. III *a, b, d*), I could have done nothing on the Theseion, and to Mr B. H. Hill and Mr G. P. Stevens I am indebted for many wise suggestions and helpful advice.

When far advanced in this research I learned that in the U.S.A. Professor Sterling Dow, of Harvard, was engaged on a parallel study of ancient roofing. On inquiry, however, it transpired that our studies were complementary rather than parallel, for Professor Dow was studying the development of roofing throughout ancient times, and not only in the classical Greek era, and moreover, being unable to visit the Mediterranean, was compelled to work only from the publications. We have corresponded frequently on the subject; however, none of Professor Dow's ideas or conclusions are embodied in the present work.

Finally, I should like to acknowledge my debt to the anonymous New Yorker who stole my luggage from my car while it was parked in Manhattan, and got away with all my site notes and photographs; for, though his initiative has resulted in some of the pictures being perforce reproduced from rather smudgy prints instead of the negative, he has given me an excellent excuse with which to cover up the many blunders of my own that doubtless lie hid within this book.

A. T. H.

CAMBRIDGE
October 1958

ABBREVIATIONS

In addition to the common abbreviations the following are used:

Aegina   A. Furtwangler, *Aegina: Das Heiligtum der Aphaia.*

Choisy   A. Choisy, *Histoire de l'architecture*, vol. I.

Cockerell   C. R. Cockerell, *The Temples of Jupiter at Aegina and Apollo at Bassae.*

Dinsmoor   W. B. Dinsmoor, *The Architecture of Ancient Greece*, 3rd edition.

Dyggve   E. Dyggve, *Das Laphrion, der Tempelbezirk von Kalydon.*

F de D   *Fouilles de Delphes.*

F de Dél   *Fouilles de Délos.*

K & P   R. Koldewey and O. Puchstein, *Die griechischen Tempel in Unteritalien und Sicilien.*

L & S   Liddell and Scott, *Greek-English Lexicon.*

Olympia   E. Curtius, F. Adler, and others, *Olympia: Die Ergebnisse der vom Deutschen Reich veranstalteten Ausgrabungen.*

P & C   G. Perrot and C. Chipiez, *Histoire de l'art dans l'antiquité*, vol. VII.

P & S   J. M. Paton and G. P. Stevens, *The Erechtheum.*

Penrose   F. C. Penrose, *Principles of Athenian Architecture.*

Plommer   W. H. Plommer, *Three Attic Temples* (B.S.A. 1950).

RD   A. T. Hodge, *A Roof at Delphi* (B.S.A. 1954).

SIG   *Sylloge Inscriptionum Graecarum*, 3rd edition, edited by Dittenberger.

EXPLANATION OF TERMS

One of the results of the somewhat inadequate study accorded the subject is a correspondingly inadequate vocabulary of technical terms; I therefore give a glossary of all whose meaning might be ambiguous, together with a number of new ones that I have been forced to coin in order to avoid frequent and tedious repetition.

BATTENS. Light wooden members laid on top of the rafters and at right angles to them (see Fig. 15).

CLOSED (OPEN) SOCKET. A closed socket is one where the stonework closes in on top so as to form a roof to the socket; conversely, an open socket is one that is carried up to the limit of the stonework so as to permit the beam to be dropped into place from above. See Fig. 1 for open (*a*) and closed (*b*) sockets.

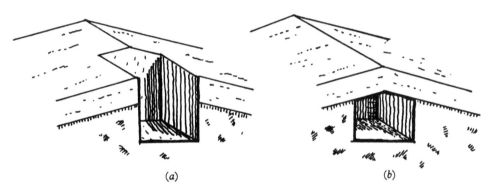

(*a*)   (*b*)

Fig. 1. Open and closed sockets.

CROSSBEAM. A heavy beam laid across between the side walls of a building and supporting a load placed vertically upon it. In some books it is called a bearer beam. I do not use the term of the lowest member of a triangular tie-beam truss.

DOVETAILED SOCKET. A socket that is wider at the back than at the mouth (see p. 94 and Fig. 9).

FLAT (SLOPING) TOPPED CORNICE BLOCK. A side cornice the top of which is flat (or sloping) across the whole width of the entablature (see p. 77).

EXPLANATION OF TERMS

GAGGERA ROOF. A roof structure on the lines of that of the Megaron of Demeter at Gaggera. It is characterized by a great number of small, tilted purlins, which can sometimes be set under the tile joints (see pp. 50 ff. and Fig. 12).

PRIMARY TIMBERS. The ridge beam and purlins. This does not include the various props required to support them.

PROP-AND-LINTEL. The traditional Greek roofing system, consisting of a crossbeam on top of which are erected vertical props to hold up the roof (see p. 35).

PURLIN. A beam laid parallel to the ridge beam and supporting the rafters and/or tiles.

ROOF. The tiles and all the woodwork required to support them. It does not include the ceiling, except in so far as that may sometimes be an integral part of the roofing construction. Much confusion has been caused in both ancient and modern writers by failure to differentiate clearly between the ceiling and the roof (for example, when Lawrence (*Greek Architecture*, p. 180) says that at one period Concord at Agrigento had a pitched roof over the cella (which is obvious) what he means is that it also had a pitched ceiling).

SECONDARY TIMBERS. Everything coming between the primary timbers and the tiles; that is, rafters, battens, sheathing, clay, rushes; or as many of these constituents as are used in the building under consideration.

SHEATHING. Light boarding laid on top of the battens and at right angles to them, that is, parallel to the rafters (see Fig. 15).

SLOT CEILING. A type of wooden ceiling the beams of which are set so close together as to leave free between them only a series of narrow slots, covered by boarding laid on top (see Appendix I, pp. 101 ff.).

THRANOS. The outermost beam of the ceiling across the end peristyle. It supports one side of the outermost bay of coffers, and lies alongside the side cornice blocks. There are other members commonly known as thranoi, but I shall use the term exclusively of the one in this position (see Fig. 6).

TILTED PURLIN. A purlin set not with its sides perpendicular, as was usual, but at right angles to the roof slope; as, for example, at Sounion and at the Megaron of Demeter at Gaggera.

WEDGE BLOCK. A wedge-shaped block laid on top of a flat-topped cornice block. Sometimes it is fairly small, sometimes it extends right across to the inside face of the entablature, making it sloping-topped (see pp. 83 ff.).

PART I
PARTICULAR EXAMPLES

I

THE TEMPLE OF POSEIDON, PAESTUM

It is always risky to quote any building as a 'typical example' of anything, for almost every structure has some peculiarity or eccentricity to be found in it somewhere; but it can safely be said that the Temple of Poseidon at Paestum is at any rate one of the most typical and certainly best preserved examples of Greek classical roofing.

Despite its excellent state of preservation, however, it has suffered the fate of most Greek buildings in South Italy in being somewhat ill published. The fullest publication is, as one would expect, in K & P (pl. IV and pp. 24–31), and there is a full restoration of the roofing woodwork in P & C, pl. VI. Neither of these works considers the roofing in detail, and the restoration by P & C, though accurate in the main, is not above suspicion on one or two points.

There are three main sources of evidence: the inside colonnade (Pl. I*b*); the inner faces of both pediments, which carry the cuttings for the primary timbers (Pl. II*a*); and the side cornice blocks, carrying the cuttings for the ends of the rafters (Pl. I*a*).

The internal colonnade is in places preserved to its full height. The upper architrave has a hawksbeak carved along its top edges, so we may be sure that the ceiling came immediately above. This gives a level for the ceiling of the cella somewhat above that over the peristyle, which is marked by the recesses cut for the ceiling beams in the inner face of the entablature (see Fig. 2). As usual, there is no evidence how the cella ceiling was constructed, for, being of wood, it has completely disappeared. It is just possible that the architraves of the inside colonnade still carry some trace of the beams laid on them, but I was able to inspect them only from on top of the side cornice; from there their tops looked very worn and irregular, with no visible beam marks. It will be seen that I have restored a coffered ceiling. The cuttings for the peristyle ceiling indicate a peculiar one, without parallel, of wide planks spaced far apart, with the gaps in between presumably boarded over. Something of the same sort may also have been used over the cella, but ceilings were not necessarily the same throughout a temple,[1] and so I chose coffers as they seem to have been the type most widely used.

Both pediments preserve the cuttings for the primary timbers. There was a ridge beam, and, the temple being a large one, four instead of the usual two purlins,[1] aligned over the internal colonnade and the cella walls. The two pairs of purlins are not, however, of the same dimensions, for the inner pair are much deeper and narrower than the outer,[2] and from this difference we may make certain deductions. The first point to note is that, as often, the sockets do not necessarily represent the size of the actual beams. The sockets are open and come right up to the top of the raking cornice blocks, that is to say, to tile level. The beams, however, should have stopped some distance below this to leave room for the rafters to be laid on top of them. The secondary timbers, as can be measured from the cuttings for them along the side cornice, were 29 cm. thick. This amount, subtracted from the total height of the primary cuttings, should give the height of the actual primary timbers. This gives a ridge beam of cross-section 67 × 74 cm., and the inner purlins 48 × 74 cm. Now the normal classical Greek rule for heavy timbers was to make them more or less square, like the ridge beam and rafters[3] of this same temple; they could, it is true, be rather higher than they were broad, but proportions of 48 cm. broad by 74 cm. high are distinctly unusual,[4] paralleled only by the temple of Aphaia (see pp. 50 f.). They are none the less structurally sound and perfectly possible; the outer purlins present a more serious problem.

The cuttings for them are 74 × 83 cm. The subtraction of 29 cm. for the secondary timbers leaves dimensions of 74 cm. wide by 54 cm. high (indeed, only 25 cm. high on the low side) for the actual beam. If the inner purlin was too high for its width, this one has gone to the opposite extreme, and for a major structural member these dimensions are quite impossible. The only way we can restore a beam of normal proportions is by utilizing the whole cutting for the beam and neglecting the secondary timbers. This will give a beam of 74 × 83 cm., which is reasonable enough. The absence of the secondary timbers over these beams can be explained, and only explained, if the rafters, instead of being carried on across on top of the beams as usual, were rabbeted into notches cut in the sides of them. This is the significance of the different sizes of purlin cutting: the outer purlin is wide because it is a major beam, and shallow because it could be set high through the rafters being set into the sides of it; the inner purlin is narrow because it is not so important a beam, and deep-set because it had to be sunk to let the rafters pass over the top of it. P & C, who do not seem to have studied the timbers in detail, rabbet the rafters into each side of the

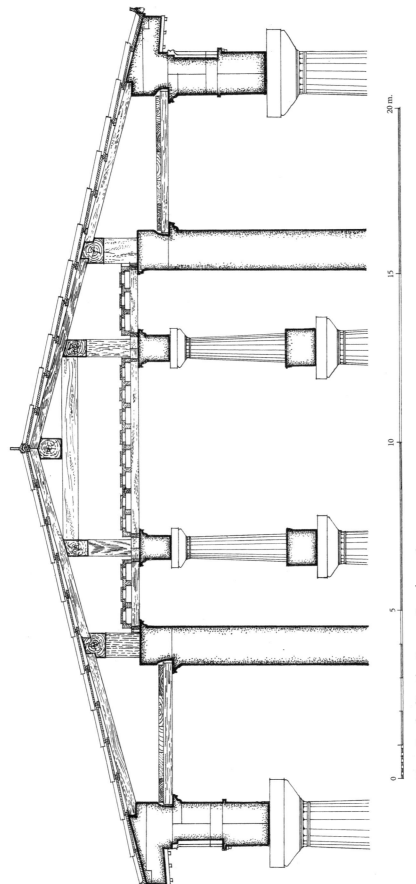

0   5   10   15   20 m.

Fig. 2. Temple of Poseidon, Paestum. General restoration.

inner purlin also, but in view of the depth of the cutting this seems unlikely. They also show both pairs of purlins as being the same size.

We must now consider the functions of the two pairs of purlins as conceived by the architect. The chief difference is that while the heavier outer purlin is thought of as supporting the ends of two separate and independent sections of roof, one on either side, the inner purlin is thought of as a prop under an existing roof that has rather too long a span and needs support.

Now it is always easiest to roof a building by laying the timbers in the direction that has the shortest span. Over the pronaos and end peristyle of any temple the shortest span is that along the axis of the building; the most natural form of roof for this part of a temple, considered separately from the rest, is therefore some form of Gaggera roof (see pp. 50 f.) with most of its members running across in the direction of the shortest span. Here, however, the chief purpose of the purlins seems to be to break up into manageable portions the long span, that across the temple— hence the break between two independent roofs over the outer purlin and the prop under the rafters at the inner one. It is the span from ridge to eaves that the architect had in mind when designing this part of the building, not the shorter span from pediment to crosswall. There can be only one explanation of his employing over the end peristyle a system so unnatural and inconvenient: he was carrying through, for the sake of uniformity, the system employed over the cella, where, of course, the ridge-to-eaves span was the shortest. Thus, although none of the inter-mediate crosswalls is preserved high enough to give evidence of the system of roofing used, I think we may assume with reasonable security that the disposition of the primary timbers over the cella corresponded to the spacing of the sockets in the pediments.[1]

Having thus established the level of the ceiling over the cella and the spacing of the primary timbers we must now turn our attention to the area lying between the two. For this we are reduced to guesswork pure and simple. The problem is, of course, how were the primary timbers supported? The outer purlins are simple enough. They are centred over the cella wall and so could be supported either on a row of vertical wooden props along the top of it or on the wall itself carried up to roof level.[2] P & C restore the latter. The objections to it are twofold. First, wooden props would be infinitely cheaper to provide and easier to erect than coursed masonry. They would also be no less effective. Second, P & C show as the top course of the wall a row of blocks with their tops cut to the slope of the roof and with rafter sockets running in on both sides; and I have never seen such a block either at Paestum or anywhere else. If this form of construction were in general use—and P & C quote Paestum as a typical example of temple roofing—then trace of it should be found somewhere. For these reasons I have restored wooden props.

The inner purlins also are straightforward for, being centred over the inner colonnade, more props are all that is required. But the ridge beam sets a problem. There are two possibilities. First, it could have been supported on vertical props, from the middle of the ceiling beams, which, of course, would have to be of fairly heavy proportions such as 60 cm. square or thereabouts. This solution is adopted by Choisy, p. 436. However, inspection of Fig. 2 reveals another possibility. The top of the inner purlins, it will be seen, is just level with the bottom of the ridge beam. Thus a cross member rabbeted into the purlins would pass directly below the ridge beam, which would be supported on it without the need of any intermediate prop or block.[1] The coincidence in level of the top of the purlins and the bottom of the ridge beam is striking and might be thought conclusive were it not that the same relationship can be observed between the outer and inner purlins, where, since there can be no question of a crossbeam, it must be fortuitous.

In the absence of all material evidence we are driven back on conjecture in our attempt to decide between these two alternatives. Of the two, the second is probably the sounder structurally; the roof is bonded more closely together by a cross member joining purlins and ridge beam than it would be if the ridge beam were supported on a row of tall vertical props. On the other hand, the first might be preferable if the attic between ceiling and roof was to be used for any kind of ceremony, for it encumbers the space less. There are, of course, few aspects of classical architecture about which we know less than the uses of the attic. Our temple had a set of stairs leading to the attic, so it was certainly used; but what for? If only for storage or maintenance inspection of the roof, then a cumbersome (but sound) system would be acceptable. If, however, it was required for some form of ceremony then the more spacious form of construction might be preferred.

Now it seems likely that in the temple of Concord at least (see p. 30) the attic was in ceremonial use. It seems equally likely that in many of the temples provided with stairways it was not, for the space between ceiling and roof was often too low to allow a man to stand upright or move around in comfort.[2] With which are we dealing at Paestum? Since nothing whatever of the attic remains this is not an easy question to answer, but it is a peculiarity of the Temple of Poseidon that instead of the usual two stairways there was only one, the entrance to that on the south being a dummy.[1] The provision of two stairways in the Temple of Concord seems to show that whatever the ceremonial enacted in its attic, good access was considered

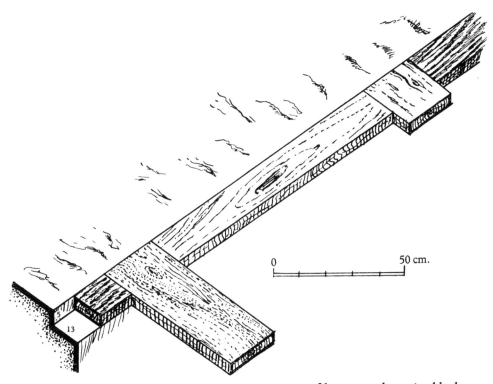

Fig. 3. Temple of Poseidon, Paestum. Arrangement of battens and cornice blocks at the inner edge of the raking cornice.

essential. Accordingly, the deliberate omission of one of them in the much larger Temple of Poseidon seems to show that no great importance was attached to ready access to the attic and that it may well have been used only for storage. This would remove all objection to the cross member between the inner and outer purlins. It should also be noted that these cross members would go far to answer another query already propounded: why were the inner purlins so deep in proportion to their width? The answer could well be to give space for rabbeting in the cross members.

Having thus dealt with all the woodwork up to the primary timbers, we must now consider the secondaries. The chief evidence is the row of sockets cut along the inside edge of each of the side cornices (Pl. I*a*). These sockets are regularly cut. They are about 29 cm. deep and 26·5 cm. wide. They are on an interaxial spacing of 101·5 cm.[1] The sockets for the rafters at each end are not preserved, but from the spacing of the others it would appear that the edge of the raking cornice blocks came half-way across the width of a tile.

A slight but continuous depression runs along the inside edge of the raking cornice blocks (Fig. 3). This I can explain only as some sort of a seating for the battens laid on top of the rafters and I have so restored it in my figure. This seating is not very deep—only about 5 cm. It may not give a very substantial batten to span the gaps between rafters on an interaxial spacing of 101·5 cm., but it is not unreasonable since the cuttings for the rafters, which are 29 cm. deep, must have the thickness of the battens (5 cm.) subtracted from them to give the thickness of the rafter itself; and a rafter less than 24 cm. deep (29−5) would be becoming out of proportion with its known width of 26·5 cm.

On top of the battens, one presumes, came the tiles—the total of 29 cm. for all the secondary woodwork leaves little room for sheathing or clay, which could be provided only at the expense of weakening the other members that supported it. The tiles were presumably of terra-cotta and at a rafter spacing of 101·5 cm., the pantiles must have been at least a full metre square—possibly their length was slightly greater. A tile of these dimensions is exceptionally large, though, of course, it is a big temple.[2] To the best of my knowledge no tiles have been definitely attributed to it.

8

II

THE THESEION

The best among the old publications of this building are those by Stuart and Revett, and Penrose, although this last does not go into any great detail. In more recent times it has been the subject of detailed study by many archaeologists; especial reference must be made to the articles by Dinsmoor,[1] who gives a comprehensive bibliography to which nothing requires to be added except the article by Plommer[2] and the recent book by Koch, *Studien zum Theseustempel in Athen*. None of these scholars has published a serious study of the roofing or attempted a restoration of it, with the exception of Plommer, who, however, being unable to get up himself to the upper parts of the building, had to rely on the publications and observations of others. My own restoration, Fig. 4, follows that of Dinsmoor[3] in all save the actual woodwork.

The main lines along which the roof of the Theseion was constructed are clear enough, but much of the detail remains puzzling.

The very prominent cuttings in the pediment (Pl. III*a*) show that the temple had a ridge beam and two purlins aligned more or less on the cella walls.

In the cella, Dinsmoor's calculations,[4] which do not need to be repeated here, result in the provision of a wooden ceiling at two different levels: a plain boarded ceiling over the narrow space between the cella wall and the inside colonnade, and the ceiling proper, some 50–60 cm. higher, over the centre of the cella. I am not particularly happy about this arrangement, but it does not affect the support of the ridge beam, with which we are here concerned. This was presumably achieved by upright props from the ceiling beams, which would be of suitably heavy timbers. A cross member between the purlins, such as I have restored in the Temple of Poseidon at Paestum, is possible but not probable; plainly a crossbeam of some sort is required for the support of the ridge beam, and it would be foolish not to take advantage of the shorter span by simply running it across the colonnade, and, having done so, to use it for the ceiling as well. I have restored a shallow coffered ceiling as one of the simplest answers to the perennial question 'What was the ceiling like?', but it remains quite conjectural.

The support of the purlins is not quite so simple a matter. Again, vertical wooden piers seem the answer, but now a discrepancy becomes apparent, for on the spacing given by the pediment sockets[1] the purlins are not centred over the cella walls but slightly overhang their inner edges.[2] This would make them rather difficult to support and I have accordingly moved them slightly outwards so that they can stand on a firm footing. This puts them some 15 cm. or so out of line with the pediment sockets, but we must remember that these give sure evidence only for the first section of the roof and that beyond the crosswall any modification to the spacing could easily be made; indeed, it is quite possible that the sockets were cut before the difficulty in the spacing was noticed. Only a slight shift would be needed, involving no structural alterations; and the various changes in design recorded by Dinsmoor[3] seem to show that the Theseion architect was not a man who worried about altering his plans as circumstances might dictate.

The purlins were about 38 cm. wide.[4] Both the south-west and south-east sockets have been cut back through the entire thickness of the tympanum backers (56 cm.), so that the back of the socket is formed by the tympanum facing slab. The cutting was not open, as at Paestum,[5] but instead was closed by the raking cornice block being laid on top like a lid. The actual purlin cutting was carried down to the course join (see Pl. III a), but the whole of the socket thus formed was not occupied by the beam, the lower part of the cutting having apparently been blocked up. In the south-west socket there is cut inside a slight step about 18 cm. from the bottom of the socket,[6] which, above the step, is rather wider. This marks the bottom of the actual beam. The north-west socket is much more peculiar. It is of more or less orthodox dimensions—39 cm. wide by 50 cm. high (measured on the low side)—save that it is surprisingly shallow, being indeed recessed at the most a mere 15 cm. in from the face of the tympanum backers, as compared with the generous 56 cm. of both the other purlin sockets and the ridge beam sockets. The actual socket is cut in two different courses, for the course join runs across the middle of it (see Pl. III a, right-hand side). The block forming the lower half of the back of the socket is thus separate from that forming the upper. The first of these two blocks is not entirely above suspicion, for it is surrounded by cement, so that it is impossible to say if it is really part of one of the tympanum backers or just a loose stone that has somehow found its way in there during some medieval rebuilding; if so, it is not impossible that the socket should have been originally much more deeply recessed. No definite answer

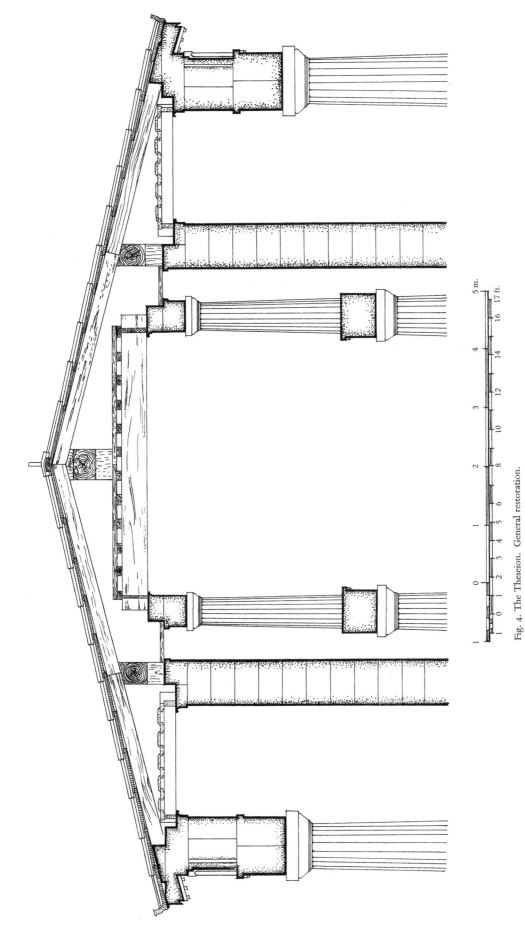

5 m.

17 ft.
16
14
12
10
8
6
5
4
3
2
1
0
1

Fig. 4. The Theseion. General restoration.

could be given without excavating through the cement. The upper of the two blocks seems to settle the matter, however, for here there is no question of medieval reconstruction. The back and left-hand side of the socket are all cut out of one of the tympanum backers, and here there is no cement to obscure the issue. Whatever

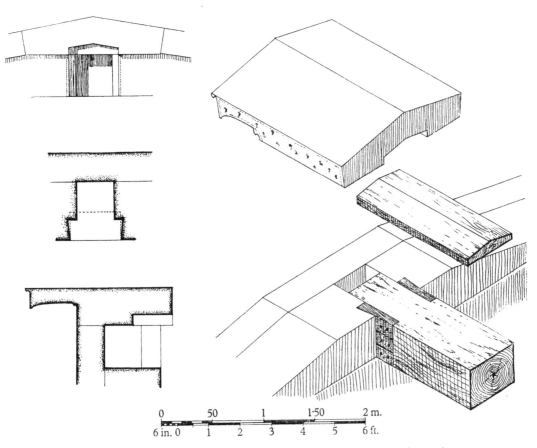

Fig. 5. The Theseion. Restoration of ridge beam (west pediment).

happened in the lower half of the socket it seems quite definite that the upper half of the north-west purlin socket of the Theseion was never recessed more than 15 cm.[1]

When we come to consider the ridge beam we again find ourselves beset by serious difficulties. The two sockets are excellently preserved, one in each pediment, and there is no difficulty about working out how much of the socket was occupied by the beam, for they are closed sockets, like those of the purlins. The aperture thus formed is more or less square[2] and of reasonable proportions for a beam. However, instead of being of plain, parallel bore throughout its depth, as was usual, the interior of each of these sockets is found to be a bewildering complex of steps, ledges, set-backs, and tapers. Both sockets are well preserved and present the same phenomenon (Pl. III*b*, Fig. 5). These complex arrangements inside the socket have not attracted any great attention hitherto. Penrose in his section (pl. 35) illustrates the socket correctly, but in such a manner that, lacking any explanation in the text, his drawing cannot be understood; Koch (*op. cit.*) illustrates the socket fully in his fig. 58, but in the text passes over it in silence. The complexities of this socket—with slight variations they are the same at each end of the temple—are easy neither to describe nor to explain. They centre around the fact that the socket is divided into two halves, one of which is cut in the top course of the tympanum backers, and the other in the apex block of the raking cornice; and, apart from their congruence at the mouth of the socket, these two halves bear no relation to each other. The top half is of parallel bore and runs back into the stone a distance of about 38 cm. (counting the 9·5 cm. that the raking cornice blocks overhang the tympanum backers). The lower half widens out as it goes back into the stone until it is 4–5 cm. wider than at the mouth; then, 20 cm. in, this wide part stops short, and an opening 41·5 cm. wide continues straight on back, parallel bore, until it meets the tympanum slab.[1]

What can be the explanation of this cutting? The taper on the lower half seems to indicate some sort of wedge to hold the beam in place, but what of the other cuttings? It would appear that the truth will most easily be found if we pass on the beam the observation already made on the socket, for if we imagine the ridge beam as a composite member consisting of two separate halves, answering to the two halves of the socket, then a solution emerges which is at least possible. This is illustrated on the right-hand side of Fig. 5. The uppermost of the two members forming the ridge beam, which is much the smaller, is accommodated in the top portion of the socket. The lower, which is the main beam, rests in the lower, secured by wedges. It will be seen that on the system I have restored the wedges could be put in position first, and then, when the main beam was slid in between them, the nails fastening the two together driven in to make the whole a single unit. This would enable the beam to be slid into place after the stonework was finished, avoiding the necessity of leaving the apex block of the cornice off so as to allow the ridge beam to be dropped into position from above.

Although this solution provides the only possible answer to the stone-cutting, it in turn raises two new questions, namely why the wedges, and why the composite beam? The normal purpose of wedges is, or should be, to hold firmly a member under tension; and it might be thought that the dovetailing of the ridge beam into the stonework might be a device to make it act as a stay arresting any tendency of the pediment to fall outwards. To ensure this the other end of the beam would have to be firmly anchored; a chain of ridge beams, all dovetailed into the various cross-walls and bonded together at their joints on the long stretch over the cella, would in theory bind the two pediments together and increase the stability of the building, but such an arrangement is improbably elaborate and complicated. I prefer to believe that the architect was anxious to have a really good and stable ridge beam and used the dovetail simply as a more secure form of joint.[1] This may also have prompted him to lay the cornice block on top of the beam to hold it firm instead of using an open socket as was more usual. He repeated this treatment at Sounion but without the wedges or composite beam.

Why then the composite beam? The first point to be noted is that the top member is much too small to have any structural importance. It cannot be that the builder could not get a single beam big enough and had to use two bolted together because, for one thing, the size required was comparatively modest—less than 50 cm. square —and, for another, if the proportions of the two constituent members were due to chance, it is unlikely that they would be duplicated so exactly and in such peculiar ratio at each end of the building. A more likely explanation is that the thin continuous cap laid on the larger beam is a device for counteracting any sag that might develop in the ridge beam. Should this occur, a few wedges driven between the two members would lift the thin cap up until it was back in the true line of the ridge and the sag compensated. This seems to me a very likely explanation in principle (I must admit I cannot in practice work out in detail a satisfactory method of driving in the wedges, owing to interference from the rafters), especially in view of the care the architect devoted, as we have seen, to making the ridge beam secure. Whether it would actually have worked I do not know, but it looks the kind of thing that might have been tried as an experiment.

So much for the ridge beam and purlins; what of the secondary timbers resting on them?

The tiles, as usual, were laid directly on top of the raking cornice blocks. The upper surface of the cornice may thus be taken as the tile level, and the space between it and the top of the ridge beam as the space available for the secondary timbers. This distance is 24 cm.[1] We must now decide of what these secondary timbers consisted, and here we are reduced to deduction from probability. This must be based mainly on calculation of the amount of space available; this, as is shown by the ridge beam, is 24 cm. This is not a particularly liberal allowance and it is instructive to compare it with the Temple of Poseidon at Paestum. There a space of 29 cm. was available, of which 5 cm. was used for the battens, giving a rafter 24 cm. thick. The longest spans to be covered in each building[2] were much the same. Paestum had larger tiles, but they were surely of terra-cotta, while the Theseion had marble tiles. A marble tile weighs fully half as much again as a terra-cotta tile of the

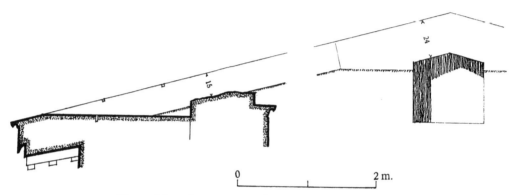

Fig. 6. The Theseion. South-west corner and ridge.

same size. These comparisons would lead one to expect in the Theseion a rafter at least equal in thickness to those of Paestum, that is 24 cm. This, however, if accepted, makes battens impossible, for all the space is needed for the rafters. I have therefore omitted battens and laid the tiles directly on the rafters.[3]

The correctness of this supposition seems to be confirmed at the four corners of the building, for there there is a bottleneck between the ceiling and the roof, leaving a very limited space for the rafters. The ceiling over the end peristyle is as usual laid with its beams parallel to the axis of the temple. At each side the thranos lies alongside the side cornice blocks. Its top also rises considerably above them, high enough to get in the way of the roof. To minimize this interference the outer top edge of the thranos, which is the point most in the way, has been completely removed, and the thranos thus given a sloping top, the slope corresponding more or less to the roof slope (Fig. 6). The rafters had to pass between this sloping top and the tiles.

This distance varies at each of the four angles of the building, for the cutting of the top of the thranos was not carefully executed—indeed, at the north-west angle (Pl. III c) it was not touched at all—but it is generally round about 15 cm., never more than 20 cm., and once is as low as 13 cm. (see Pl. III d, and Koch, *op. cit.* pls. 48, 50).

What is the significance of this narrow gap through which the rafters passed? Does 15 cm. represent the real thickness of the rafter and not the 24 cm. measured at the ridge? This cannot be, and only one explanation is possible. The rafters were of the 24 cm. indicated at the ridge, but were reduced in thickness to get them through the bottleneck. In other words, the architect found that he had no room for both the rafters and the thranos, so he took a bit off each. This bite would have to be sawn out of the bottom of the secondary timbers, which is another reason for believing that there were no battens; a really substantial rafter is required if it is to be mutilated in this way.

Such an arrangement no doubt appears unlikely at first sight, but the testimony of the stone blocks, all of which are still in their original positions, seems to allow no other solution. Moreover, only the rafters at each end of the building will be affected, for the ceiling over the side peristyle is just low enough to allow the rafters to pass at their full thickness (see Fig. 4). The difficulty arises from the architect's desire to put the ceiling as high as possible, which has brought it into conflict with the claims of the roof. This desire, though not peculiar to the Theseion architect, has left its mark on all three of the buildings attributed to him, for in all three pieces of the ceiling had to be shaved off to accommodate awkward corners of the roof. Indeed, the conflict became accentuated in his later buildings, culminating in an almost impossible situation on the side cornice at Rhamnous.[1]

It would appear that the side cornice is incomplete as it stands, for it originally had another course of small, wedge-shaped blocks laid on top. The evidence for these is twofold. First, there is a row of both dowel and pry holes along the flat top of the existing cornice blocks; second, the first block of the raking cornice at the south-west angle of the temple preserves the halves of two H-clamp cuttings; the clamps joined the cornice blocks to the missing course. These two pieces of evidence taken together make the restoration of the course reasonably safe, but its exact form is not so easy to determine.[2] The two clamp marks tell us that it was at least 72 cm. broad, and its top was presumably cut on a slope so as to fit in under the tiles and support them. I have avoided carrying the taper through into a point at the thin end of this block, a thing that the Greeks apparently never did for fear of the stone breaking. It is odd to find the stone below continuing on flat at such a junction; normally it sits up in a sort of lip, as in my restoration of the Temple of Ares (Fig. 18). At the other side of the course the rafters were presumably stopped against it. They could have been accommodated, as Dinsmoor suggests, in a row of individual sockets cut for them, as at Bassae, but the smallness of the course has led me to adopt the simpler solution, that they simply abutted against it.

Along the cornice there is also preserved a second row of dowels. These come in pairs. Each pair is 11–12 cm. apart, and the pairs are set at intervals of 1·30 m. (Plommer, p. 73, quoting Dinsmoor). This presumably means that the tiles were 65 cm. broad, a conclusion confirmed by a series of dressings found on the raking cornice of both pediments. These are very slight, and indeed only just discernible, but they were plainly made for the reception of the tiles, which, of course, were laid flat on the stonework. They take the form of a series of rectangles;[1] their outlines vary a great deal and are only roughly defined, but they agree well enough with a tile width of 65 cm., for they vary from 64 to 70 cm. in width. And if the tiles were spaced on an interval of 65 cm., so presumably were the rafters. We may therefore restore rafters 24 cm. deep by about the same width, and on an interaxial spacing of 65 cm.

III

THE MEGARON OF DEMETER, GAGGERA

The Megaron of Demeter at Gaggera has for long been recognized as a highly original building. My preliminary examination of it rapidly led me to the conclusion that its originality extended also to the roof structure, and it was only after considerable further study that I realized that the type of roof structure of which Gaggera offers so complete an example was in widespread use throughout both Sicily and mainland Greece. For this reason alone it deserves careful study.

The temple, which has been published by K & P (pp. 85–90) and later by Gabrici (*MA*, XXXII, 1927–8), is non-peripteral and divided into pronaos, cella and adyton. None of the walls are preserved to cornice height but most of the blocks vital to a reconstruction are still to be found on the site. At first sight they seem a singularly unpromising collection, for neither side nor raking cornice carry any sockets for the roofing beams. This is so because the usually reliable rule whereby we may equate tile and raking cornice level breaks down at Gaggera, where the cornice sat up above the roof like a coping, with the tiles fitting in under its back edge, which is roughly cut to a stepped line so as to fit down on them neatly. The sockets for the roof beams are instead to be sought in the tympanum blocks, and there they will be found.[1]

There are several tympanum blocks still preserving the beam sockets, all of which belong to one of two types, illustrated by the blocks *a* and *b* in Fig. 7. One type of socket, appearing on block *b*, is of the normal, straight-sided type, 11·5 cm. wide by 10·5 cm. deep, and recessed 14 cm. The other type, shown on both blocks, is larger, and also more complex in shape. In plan, the socket is strongly dovetailed, the back being some 3·5 cm. wider than the mouth. In elevation, on the other hand, it is bell-mouthed, the top of the socket being about 6 cm. wider than the bottom. This type is for a much larger beam, about 20 cm. wide by 22 cm. high, though neither could really be called heavy timbers.

It is plain that we are here dealing with two distinct roofing systems, used over two different parts of the building. This is shown by block *b*, from one of the crosswalls, which carries two of the sockets back to back. The main outline of the structure is plain enough. It consisted of a number of small and light purlins, which were tilted so as to be set at roof pitch. Block *a* shows that they were set on an interaxial spacing of 72·5 cm. This corresponds well with the tile length as given by the steps cut in under the edge of the raking cornice, so we may safely assume that these small purlins were aligned to lie one under each tile joint. Block *b* also shows that over one compartment of the building the same structure was carried on with beams much reduced in size but on the same spacing. Logic demands that the roof roofed with the small beams be either the pronaos or adyton, which have the smaller span. It cannot be both, for block *a* shows that one of the end walls of the temple had the heavier beams abutting against it. Of the two, it seems more likely that the small beams were laid over the pronaos, which has a slightly shorter span than the adyton —3·30 m. instead of 3·68 m. Block *b* is thus presumably from the crosswall between pronaos and cella, carrying sockets for the small beams over the former and the larger ones of the latter. Block *a* would be from the back wall of the adyton.

This gives a roof structure at first sight rather unconventional; certainly one very different from the two previous buildings studied. Its chief features, however, seem to be beyond dispute. There were ten small purlins and the ridge beam running the length of the building. The beam sockets were set back to back over the crosswalls so that the beams carried on the same alignment on either side but did not touch each other at the point of junction. Over the pronaos the beams were small and sat in square sockets. Over the cella and adyton they were larger and sat in a socket that was both wide at the top, so that the beam would slip into place easily, and dovetailed in plan, to ensure a firm joint.[1] Most of this is shown in the large drawing in Fig. 8, p. 23, and is reasonably certain; we must now consider the secondary timbers which, as usual, set something of a problem.

The problem chiefly lies, as in the Theseion, in lack of space. The cuttings for the purlins over the pronaos, as shown in block *b*, are very small; they are so small that I am convinced that the whole cutting must have been occupied by the beam. A member of about 11 cm. square is just enough to carry the weight of one row of tiles over a span of 3·30 m., and could not be made much smaller; yet if rafters are to be laid on top of it, to say nothing of battens and sheathing, the necessary space must be deducted from the thickness of the purlin. I therefore believe that, over the pronaos at least, there were no rafters. This revolutionary idea may perhaps

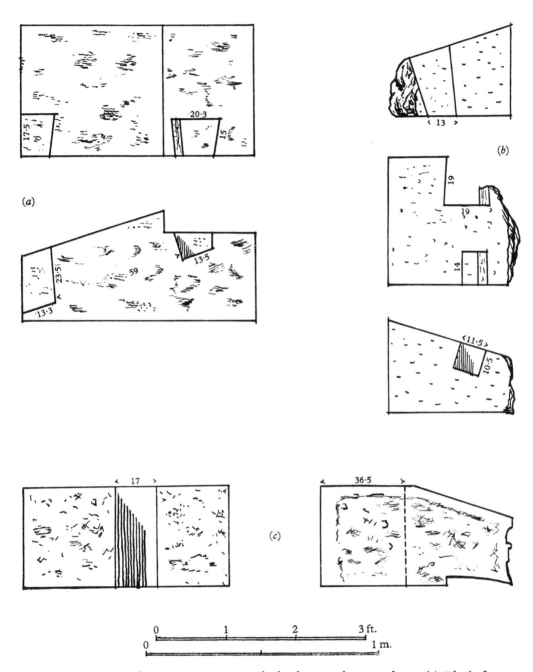

Fig. 7. Megaron of Demeter, Gaggera. Blocks showing beam sockets. (a) Block from tympanum; (b) block from crosswall; (c) side cornice block.

appear less startling when it is seen that to all intents and purposes the purlins are in fact the rafters laid sideways to take advantage of the short span, and the tiles are still supported, as usual, at their upper and lower edges.

Over the cella the position is less simple. The purlins are larger and slightly deeper than they are wide; here rafters are at least not impossible. At the same time they still cannot be very thick, for the cuttings for the purlins are only slightly deeper than they are wide, and too thick a rafter will give them an excessively flattened cross-section. The effect of this observation is to make the rafter question less important. There is room for only a very thin rafter—so thin that it will have little structural significance, being a mere lath 4 cm. or so thick. To all intents and purposes it is the purlins that will be supporting the tiles, as before. Is it then worth while restoring rafters at all?

There are two arguments in favour, neither of which is decisive. First there is the undoubted fact that, compared with the cuttings over the pronaos, those over the cella are slightly deeper in proportion to their width. Second, there is the point that over a long span any kind of cross member laid across the tops of the purlins, even a thin rafter, would help to bond the roof together and hold the purlins in their proper spacing, much as the sleepers hold the rails on a railway track. These two considerations have led me to the conclusion that there probably were rafters over the cella and adyton.

The upper surface of the side cornice blocks is flat, with no rafter cuttings to help us. However, I noticed on two of the best preserved blocks, especially that at present to be found on top of the side wall near the south-west corner of the building, a slight dressing or depression running along the top back corner of the block.[1] It is sunk about 0·75 cm. below the normal level. This was clearly cut to accommodate something. A course of masonry is out of the question, so it must have been a beam of some sort; and so I have restored a wooden wall plate with the ends of the rafters rabbeted into it.

We must now face the most serious problem presented by the building: how were the primary timbers supported over the cella? Supported they must have been, for the cella is 10·46 m. long, and the purlins only 20 cm. square. It is perhaps just conceivable that these could have supported a roof of light tiles, but most improbable. For one thing, unless some form of rafters were provided to hold them the right distance apart they would be liable, as we have noted, to warp out of their proper spacing on so long a span; and the provision of such rafters would weaken the purlins, on the same principle that led us to reject sheathing at Paestum (p. 8). Moreover, even if the purlins could in fact have supported the roof the margin of strength in hand would be impossibly narrow in comparison with what we know of Greek practice in other buildings.

It can be taken as certain that some form of intermediate support was provided, but what form? Presumably it started with a crossbeam laid across from one side of the cella to the other. The span was 8·45 m., so this would present no great difficulty. What was constructed on top of the crossbeam is less easily determined.

The traditional way of supporting a ridge beam or a purlin from a crossbeam is by a vertical prop, but this will hardly serve us here, for the idea of a row of eleven props, one to each purlin, is really rather absurd. It is practically impossible to devise any way of supporting all of these purlins individually; the only practical way is the way they are fixed to a pediment running under them all collectively; and so I am convinced that at one or more points there was erected across the cella some kind of wooden structure in the form of a triangle, on the upper sides of which the purlins rested. I can see no other way of supporting them. This triangular structure is of great importance, or would be if we could determine its precise form.

The traditional form of construction, as has been said, is one based on the erection of upright props on a crossbeam, and something of this kind is quite possible. In the first of the three reconstructions shown in Fig. 8 *b* I have restored such a system. A crossbeam is laid across between the side walls of the cella, and a prop from its midpoint supports the two long sloping timbers; these also rest on two intermediate uprights. This may well be the right answer, but another possibility of the greatest significance must not be neglected: any mention of roofing timbers arranged in triangular form is bound to call to mind the question of the truss.

The problem of when the truss came into general use in Greek architecture need not concern us here,[1] but in view of the highly suggestive probability of the triangular wooden structure we must consider whether it could have been used at Gaggera. There are two lines of approach along which we may seek to discover the truth. First, we may seek to establish from a comparison of the timbers used and the span to be crossed whether a truss would in fact be structurally necessary. Second, we may attempt to determine whether the design of the building suggests that the truss was in common use at that period. This last is not so long or arduous an undertaking as it sounds, for all that we have to consider is the row of ten small purlins over the cella. Immediately a question leaps to the eye: why are they there?

That they should be employed across the pronaos or adyton of the building is natural enough. It is a shorter span along the axis of the temple than across it, and since on each side of the room a pediment existed, what simpler than to lay the purlins across between them? But this argument breaks down completely for the cella. This was 10·64 m. long by only 8·47 m. wide, yet the architect chose to run his timbers along the longer of the two spans. Moreover, the roof of small purlins, ideal for laying across between two pediments, can only with great difficulty be supported on anything else, and we have already been forced, without considering trusses at all, to restore something very like one in order to hold them up.

All in all, it seems a rather peculiar form of construction and I can see only one likely reason why it was used over the cella. It has already been noted that some form of triangular woodwork is the structure best suited to the purlins; the converse also holds good: the purlins are a structure suitable to be combined with some form of triangular woodwork. I believe that these wooden pediments were not provided expressly to hold the purlins, but that the purlins were laid because the wooden triangles were going to be there in any case. This at any rate makes the whole structure rather more logical; we no longer have to worry about why the purlins were carried on over the cella instead of being replaced by a ridge beam and rafters, or what manner of structure was provided to hold them. If the triangular structure was already there for other reasons, then the purlins become understandable, for the erection of the wooden pediments would turn the cella in effect into a series of small rooms, each like the pronaos or adyton. But if the crossbeams were to have some triangular structure built on to them for reasons other than the support of the purlins, it can hardly be for any other reason than that trusses were in fact used to span the cella. There was, it should be pointed out, no need for them; a span of that width could have been covered by an ordinary beam; but they could well have been used because that was a form of construction well known at that period. After all, there is no especial merit in the plain crossbeam, and if the truss was known there is no reason why it should not have been used, even if it was not essential.

The other of our two lines of approach points in the same direction. Our evidence for the size of the crossbeams will be found in the side cornice blocks, into which their ends had to be recessed. Several of these are to be found bearing cuttings for

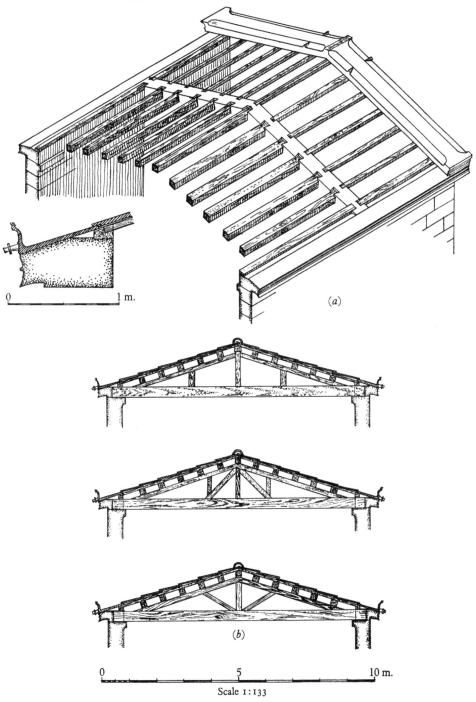

0   1 m.

(a)

(b)

0   5   10 m.

Scale 1:133

Fig. 8. Megaron of Demeter. (a) Pronaos and cella: partial restoration of woodwork.
(b) Roof over the cella: three possible systems.

23

beams, but the building was seriously damaged during conversion into a church and some of the cuttings may not be ancient.[1] Their evidence is far from conclusive, but although the cuttings permit a beam of maximum height 40·5 cm., the fact that none of the preserved parts of the cuttings is wider than 27·5 cm. suggests that the cuttings may not have been utilized to their full extent. Even assuming that they were, this will give a beam only 40 cm. high by 30 cm. wide. This is not too generous an allowance for a beam carrying all the weight of the roof over a span of 8·45 m., but, of course, it would be ample if the beam were part of a truss.

Even more peculiar is the block illustrated as *c* in Fig. 7. This is the only cornice block with a beam socket completely preserved, and the socket though 40·5 cm. high is very narrow indeed, a mere 17 cm. wide. This at first sight suggests an advanced knowledge of engineering, for it would seem that the builder had grasped the principle that the strength of a beam lies in its depth. If so, however, there would be no need of the wider sockets of which we have been speaking,[2] which seem to point to beams of the normal square cross-section. I therefore believe that the cutting in block *c* is for a small, light beam about 17 cm. square, the cutting being, as usual, carried up to the top of the block regardless of the actual size of the beam, and that the main crossbeams were about 30 cm. wide by 40 cm. high.

These two conclusions combined have led me to the belief that there were two, possibly three, trusses erected across the cella and supporting the roof. It may seem improbable that a provincial architect should understand the principle of the truss at this time, but throughout this restoration I have had regard only to the internal evidence of the building itself without considering such general aspects (for which see pp. 38 ff.). I have accordingly restored trusses in the two lower drawings shown in Fig. 8 *b*. The bottom one shows the normal type of truss, the middle one an alternative form in contemporary use today which is also attested by the Etruscan urn lid shown in Pl. VIII *c* (see p. 59).

Little remains now for us to restore except the ceiling, and about this I have no suggestions to offer, in the almost total absence of evidence. The fact that a rudimentary epikranitis was provided indicates that there probably was a ceiling, over the cella at least. Presumably the narrower beams, for one of which block *c* carries a socket,[3] formed part of it, but in the absence of any cuttings or dressings I do not feel justified in adding further to the already considerable proportion of conjecture in my restoration.

IV

THE TEMPLE OF CONCORD, AGRIGENTO

Like the Temple of Poseidon at Paestum, this temple has been the object of rather less critical attention than its state of preservation warrants, for in one point it is unique: it is the only Greek building in which any of the 'inside pediments'—that is, the crosswalls of cella, pronaos, and opisthodomos—are preserved. The only element lacking that could have contained evidence of value to our study is the side cornice, which has disappeared completely. Of it K & P (p. 174) remark 'Die Blöcke von der Langseite, von denem im Norden noch einige am Boden liegen', but none of the blocks are any longer to be found, either *in situ* or on the ground. The profile is known from the angle blocks, all four of which remain in place, but this is of little importance in a study of roofing, where the point of interest is the top inside edge of the cornice blocks, carrying the sockets for the rafters; and of this nothing remains. Fortunately, K & P publish a rudimentary plan of some of the cornice blocks, still extant in their day (K & P, fig. 152, below). They also publish a restored plan of the roof woodwork (K & P, fig. 156), but this is marred by one pardonably wrong guess and one glaring error of fact.

The first glance at either of the pediments gives one a good idea of the system of roofing, which was the same over each of the end peristyles. The pediment carries eleven cuttings for the primary timbers.[1] In the middle is the ridge beam, 36 cm. wide by 42 cm. high.[2] Of the remaining ten purlins, the two outer are much larger than the rest, being 52 cm. wide by 62 cm. high. The remaining eight, four on each side of the building, are spaced at more or less equal distances between the outer purlins and the ridge beam; unlike either of these members, they are tilted. The size of the beam varies; the depth remains constant at about 34 cm., for the sockets are carried down to and terminate at the bottom of the raking cornice, so that the beams actually rest on the course below; but the width varies from 36 cm. to 56 cm.[3]

The eleven beams contained in these sockets spanned the end peristyle and terminated in the crosswall built up over the pronaos columns. From the other side of it another set of beams (presumably the same number but not corresponding closely in spacing) ran to the next crosswall, that between pronaos and cella. Of these two crosswalls, that over the pronaos is no longer preserved above ceiling level, and has no evidence to offer. That at the east end of the cella remains standing to its full height, but has so suffered from the weather and the medieval architects who re-roofed the temple[1] that on its east face only four of the cuttings for the primary timbers are discernible, being those for four of the small purlins.

These four cuttings, however, make one thing abundantly clear: the same beams did not run through from pediment to crosswall, for the cuttings are not in line. Plainly the roofs over the end peristyle and the pronaos were independent units, and though the same number of beams were presumably used, their positions did not correspond (see Fig. 9c). Of these four cuttings three are almost in line with their counterparts in the pediment, or at any rate no more than 20 cm. out, but one, the southernmost, when compared with the cuttings in the pediment, falls into line with the gap between the middle pair of small purlins. The thickness of the cross-wall over the pronaos columns, on which these two sections of roof met, can be roughly calculated from the thickness of the entablature over the columns, less an allowance on each side for the ceiling beam ledge. This does not give a very thick wall—about 75 cm. or so—but it is thick enough to take a row of sockets cut out of either side of it. In fact, the lowest part of this wall is preserved (Pl. Vb), but I was unable to measure it. The wall over the east end of the cella was even thinner, being only 50 cm. (approx.) thick.

This then was the form of the primary timbers over the pronaos, opisthodomos, and that part of the end peristyle that lies between the antae—a heavy purlin carrying on the line of the cella wall, then four lighter but still substantial purlins, then the ridge beam. This is very reminiscent of the form of construction that we found in the Megaron of Demeter at Gaggera, and here also we are faced with the problem of how much space to allow for the secondary timbers. The total depth of all the woodwork, primary and secondary, is shown by the cuttings for the small purlins to have been 34 cm. With the average width of these purlins about 37 cm. this allows very little space for secondary members; otherwise the small purlins will become too shallow for their width. Room might be found to put in a layer of very thin rafters but nothing else. Battens or clay are out of the question. The question thus resolves itself into one of whether rafters were laid on top of these small purlins, or whether

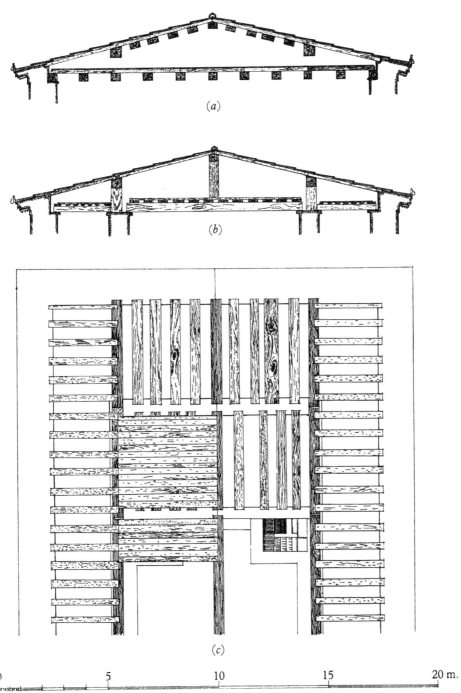

(a)

(b)

(c)

0   5   10   15   20 m.

Fig. 9. Temple of Concord, Agrigento. (*a*) Section across east peristyle.
(*b*) Section across cella. (*c*) Plan at cornice level.

the tiles lay on them directly, as I have restored at Gaggera. This is a most difficult problem to decide. It is also one of great importance, for it is much more than the minor structural point that it appears to be.

First let us consider the roof over the side peristyle. K & P's plan tells us that it was roofed with rafters about 33 cm. wide, and, one presumes, spaced on the joints of the cornice blocks, that is, every 80 cm. The other ends of these rafters would be notched into the two large outer purlins, or laid on top of them. The system was probably much the same (as we shall see) over the cella. It might have been thought more natural to carry the rafters through to the ridge over the end peristyle; this would make for uniformity of construction. Moreover, if we are to omit the rafters over these parts of the building, on the analogy of Gaggera, then the tiles must be laid direct on the small purlins. This is difficult, for in one important point they do not agree with the purlins of Gaggera—they do not have a regular spacing.

We have already noticed how these small purlins are laid only roughly in position. Now if the tiles are to be laid direct on the purlins, obviously one condition must be fulfilled: there must be purlins, if not actually centred under the tile joints, at any rate so placed as to have part of their surface under them. It is just possible that with a tile of the right size this condition could be fulfilled in spite of the higgledy-piggledy spacing of the purlins, on account of the overlap between them; but it would mean some of the tile joints falling very near to the edges of the beams, and it would have required very careful siting of the beams to make sure that they were under the joints at all. The obvious question then arises, if this careful measurement had to be undertaken, then why were the beams not aligned on the tile joints, as at Gaggera? There is no answer to this query, and we are driven to the conclusion that whoever was responsible for the siting of the small purlins did not consider the siting of the tile joints. This seems to be good evidence for the existence of rafters. If these were laid on top, the irregular spacing of the purlins would be perfectly understandable, as they would have to support a continuous rafter instead of supporting tiles at fixed intervals.

By these arguments we may deduce the presence of rafters; but soon we shall find ourselves in difficulties again, for if there were rafters, then why all the small purlins? The span from ridge to cella wall is about the same as that over the side peristyle: why not then treat it in the same way? Why not run rafters of reasonable size from ridge to outer purlin and omit the small purlins altogether? Indeed, the closer we examine these small purlins the more remarkable they seem to be. Their most remarkable feature is their enormous and quite unnecessary strength. If they were to support the roof, they should be logically more or less of the same size as the ordinary rafters. Instead, we find cuttings on an average 34 × 38 cm., with one as wide as 56 cm.,[1] and sometimes less than their own width apart. These proportions are most peculiar. The beams are far too big,[2] and far too close together. True, the Greeks seem often to have used more wood than was actually required by the strict rule of engineering—cf. the *Athenian Treasury at Delphi* (RD, figs. 6, 9)—but they seldom went to the length of providing what in places amounts to an almost continuous deck of woodwork 34 cm. thick, in order to support only a layer of terracotta tiles.

It has already been pointed out how a rafter must lead to a thinner small purlin. It is plain that any such reduction will not affect the stability of the building, for the purlins are far stronger than they need be, but it will make them very shallow in proportion to their breadth, and pose the question 'Why not a smaller and squarer beam?'. It is at all events plain that the small purlins carrying the roof over the pronaos, opisthodomos, and end peristyle are much more substantial—in particular are much wider—than necessary, and present a serious problem. I think I know the answer to this problem, but I cannot prove it.

The clue to the truth is to be found in the two crosswalls still standing, that over the east end of the cella, and that over the columns of the opisthodomos. Each of these is preserved up to roof level and is pierced by a doorway in the form of a flat-topped arch (Pl. IV *a*, *b*). Two stairways gave access to the attic space over the cella, and these doorways apparently gave further access to the attics over the rest of the temple.[3] There is, of course, nothing unusual in stairways being provided in the cella, and though this is the only building where there is definite evidence that the attics over the pronaos and opisthodomos were in use too, there is no reason to believe that such an arrangement was uncommon. Closer inspection reveals that these two doorways are bordered by a simple moulding, a plain fillet following the sides of the doorway and arching over into a point above it. This is neither unimportant nor easily explained.

It is usually stated that the attic over the cella of a temple was provided with stairways in order to allow it to be visited for purposes of storage or roof maintenance. If this is correct, we are faced with two difficulties at Agrigento. One is the provision of not one but two stairways, which seem to have been built to ensure ease of access not only for the occasional visits to check the soundness of the timbers, but for people in greater numbers. The provision of the two stairways,[1] in fact, seems to point to the attic being no mere loft, but an integral part of the temple.

This conclusion is confirmed by the moulding round the attic doorways.[2] The inference is plain, for decoration of any sort, even a rudimentary form like this, is never provided unless it is meant to be seen; and clearly we must deduce that the attic space in our temple was used for some purpose much more important than inspection or storage.[3] What that purpose was one can only guess, but one presumes that it was some kind of religious ceremony—possibly the sort of thing that took place in the adyton that is so characteristic a feature of Sicilian temples but which is lacking here.

The stairways and the mouldings together tell us that the attic was a room of importance, and indeed of somewhat ceremonial character. This explains the size of the small purlins. Their function is not only to support the roof; they are also the ceiling of the attic. When this is realized the whole problem is changed, for it is no longer enough to restore a system of woodwork that will support the tiles. It must also be acceptable as a ceiling when viewed from below. Bearing this in mind we find the shape of the small purlins much easier to understand.

The form of wooden ceiling most commonly restored is that employing wooden coffers, but there is no possibility of that here. A scarcely less common form, however, is the one that I have entitled the slot ceiling (see Appendix I). The chief feature of this is the use of ceiling planks laid close together, the slots between being boarded over on top. The resemblance between this type of ceiling and the effect that emerges if we lay light rafters on top of the small purlins is striking (cf. Fig. 9a and Fig. 21). From this I deduce that not only were rafters laid on top of the small purlins but that they were laid in a continuous deck, instead of simply one under each tile joint, which would leave the tiles visible from the attic below. This would of course be done only to provide a good ceiling and not for any structural reasons.[4]

This solution also provides an answer to the problems that have arisen over the excessive strength of the purlins and the unduly thin cross-section that they develop if rafters are added on top, for the guiding consideration was not only strength but also appearance; it is perhaps surprising that if these beams were to form a decorative ceiling they were not more regularly spaced; the only parallel is afforded by the irregularity of the beam cuttings over the peristyle of the Temple of Poseidon at Paestum, particularly across the ends, but that is possibly the result of a change in plan. The west end seems to have had seven beams and the east end six. Moreover, some of the irregularity at Paestum may be due to the sockets becoming enlarged by natural erosion, for I have not examined them at close quarters.

Thus I believe my theory at Agrigento to be correct, and the cuttings for the beams that I have referred to as the small purlins to be the last traces of a most interesting structural hybrid, formed by cross-breeding between a slot ceiling and a Gaggera roof.

We have now dealt with the roof over the pronaos, opisthodomos (which corresponds to that over the pronaos), and end peristyle, and it is time to consider that over the cella. For this we have no positive evidence whatever, but from consideration of what was most probable, and from one important piece of negative evidence, we may at least make an intelligent guess. The piece of negative evidence referred to is most interesting. K & P, p. 176, remark that it is uncertain whether the system of woodwork of the pronaos was also carried on over the cella, or it was roofed with rafters laid direct from ridge to cella wall, in the same way as the side peristyles. They apparently thought the first alternative the more likely of the two, for they dotted it in on their restored plan of the woodwork. This cannot be right. The crosswall over the east end of the cella carries on its east face cuttings for four of the small purlins over the pronaos; on its west face it carries nothing but the medieval cuttings. The evidence is quite definite. Whatever the construction of the roof over the cella it did not include the small purlins, or indeed any beam laid parallel to the axis of the building.[1] One is thus driven to the other alternative, that the cella was roofed on the same plan as the peristyle.

We cannot, however, simply lay a second set of rafters in continuation of those of the peristyle. It may have been done, but if I have rightly guessed the form of the roof over the pronaos it is unlikely, for if the attic over the pronaos had some form of ceiling, then presumably so did that over the cella. We have few clues to the reconstruction of the ceiling. The simplest form would be to lay the rafters in a continuous deck so that the tiles would be invisible from below, and this I have done (Fig. 9 c, left). This gives a ceiling very bare as seen from below, but it could be decorated in various ways, for example, by nailing on laths in a criss-cross pattern to form shallow imitation coffers; after all, they would only be seen in very subdued light.[2]

31

The next question is the support of the ridge beam. Here again there is no evidence, but there surely can be little doubt about the answer. The only possible form of construction is surely crossbeams laid across the top of the cella and supporting the ridge beam by means of vertical props. The span of the cella, 7·55 m. (K & P, pl. xxv), is small enough to cause no difficulty, and the only other possibility, some form of truss, seems unlikely. A series of tie-beams across between the purlins would so clutter up the attic as to make it uninhabitable. The crossbeam and prop construction, on the other hand, leaves the attic free except for a row of posts down the middle.

The crossbeams would also naturally carry the ceiling of the cella.[1] For this again there is no evidence, so I have restored a slot ceiling. I was prompted to do this by a desire to provide a ceiling that would both look decorative when viewed from below and provide a smooth floor that could be walked on for the attic above.[2]

The cuttings in the cornice blocks illustrated by K & P cannot be relied on to give the rafter spacing accurately. The sockets seem to occur regularly on the join of the cornice blocks, which gives a spacing of 80 cm.; but we cannot be sure, and one of the blocks published carries the socket cut not in the edge but in the middle of the block. However, assuming 80 cm. to be the correct spacing—the odd block could be explained if all the cornice blocks did not conform to the standard size; the evidence is really insufficient, and since even the blocks found by K & P have disappeared we are unlikely ever to know more—we find it possible to fit this in if we restore a rafter half the normal width alongside the raking cornice. The rafter spacing will also be that of the tiles, so we may now guess at the size of the pantiles. They would be 80 cm. wide; the distance from the cornice hawksbeak to the ridge is about 9·15 m. Thus if there were ten rows of tiles they would be set on a spacing of 91·5 cm.; if there were nine, it would be 101·7 cm. Adding 8 cm. to each to allow for the overlap between rows we get alternative figures of 99·5 cm. and 109·7 cm. for the length of the tile itself. Of the two I think the former the more probable length for a tile 80 cm. wide. According to Professor Griffo, the Superintendent of Antiquities at Agrigento, no fragments of actual tiles have been found.

PART II
GENERAL FEATURES

V

THE CEILING AND THE ATTIC

We have now studied in detail the roofing of four particular buildings, none of them without evidence of value to the study of roofing as a whole. Now, however, we must take the broader view and attempt to form some opinion of the general practice and principles of Greek roofing as a whole. It will be most convenient if we work systematically up through the various timbers, from ceiling to ridge, commencing with the ceiling.

The ceiling over the cella of a Greek temple was invariably wooden. This affects the present study in that we are forced to fall back almost entirely on conjecture in our efforts to restore it. There are two types of wooden ceiling known to have been in widespread use: the coffered ceiling[1] and the slot ceiling. I have yet to find a peripteral building in which the stonework gives a clear indication of what type of ceiling was employed over the cella, but traces of the ceiling beams are often preserved on the inside face of the side cornice of treasuries and other small buildings. Thus the Sicyonian Treasury at Olympia bears traces of a slot ceiling, the Doric Treasury at Marmaria apparently had coffers, and the Treasury of Gela at Olympia had some kind of boarded ceiling.[2] The ceiling of the cella, or any other part of the building, interests us in this study in so far as its beams could be used to support the roof.

It seems indisputable that this was often done. The average cella was much too long for the ridge beam to span unsupported. Jeffery[3] has suggested that it might be supported by an exceptionally heavy set of rafters propping each other up at the ridge, after the principle of a step ladder. All other systems involve, somehow or other, a horizontal beam laid across the top of the cella. Indeed, there are only two worth considering. The first is the truss. In its very simplest form this requires only two stout rafters fixed together at their heads and with their feet securely joined by a tie-beam, so as to form a triangle. The second, which I believe to have been most generally used, is the more traditional structure that we may, for brevity's sake, refer to as prop-and-lintel. It is formed by laying a beam across the cella and erecting a prop to the ridge from its mid-point.

3-2

Both these systems involve the use of a beam laid across the cella, as does that of Jeffery when applied to large buildings. It is in any case necessary to lay beams across the cella to form a basis for the ceiling, so it is but natural that one beam should sometimes serve both purposes and the ceiling become an integral part of the roof structure. This, it seems certain, was the rule in small buildings of treasury size. The most powerful argument is the fact that in such buildings once the ceiling is laid there is no room for a second layer of crossbeams to support the roof, which must have rested, in some way or other, on the ceiling beams.[1] The Sicyonian Treasury at Olympia is a building of interest, for it had a slot ceiling with the beams running across the building (see Appendix I, pp. 101 f.). Were these beams strong enough to bear the weight of the ridge beam? They were 25 cm. deep, and the span is 5·21 m. This is a borderline case. In actual fact, there would be an ample margin of strength, but the Greeks were always given to using very heavy timbers. I suppose that if there were any qualms, it would be easy enough to make those beams carrying the props heavier than the rest; no difference would be visible from below, and we have too few cornice blocks to permit us to be dogmatic.

Was this unity of ceiling and roof structure also the rule in large peripteral buildings? I believe that it was the rule, but not by any means the invariable rule. The largest of the four buildings to which special study was devoted, the temple at Paestum, did not conform to it, according to my reconstruction, for I have restored two rows of crossbeams, one carrying the ridge beam, and one the ceiling (Fig. 2). The reasons for this have been partly explained, but to go into them fully we must now climb up from the ceiling into that most obscure and enigmatic part of the entire Greek temple, the attic.

Of it practically nothing is known, for in only one building, the Temple of Concord at Agrigento, is anything of it preserved at all. We must, however, try to form some opinion on its purpose, for until we know whether it was officially one of the rooms of the temple or a mere loft we cannot decide whether any given roofing structure should be discarded on the grounds that it would obstruct movement in the attic. We may begin by surveying the evidence, which is very scanty. There is the evidence of the moulding round the doors at Agrigento, already discussed (pp. 29 f.). There is the statement of Pausanias[2] that in the Temple of Zeus at Olympia there was a stairway to the roof. There are beam cuttings in the lower architrave of the internal colonnade of the Temple of Aphaia, showing that there were galleries over the side aisles and access at any rate to that level by a ladder. There are a great many buildings, mostly in Sicily and Magna Graecia, with remains of stone stairways which often, in the absence of internal colonnades, must have led to the attic. Of these the Temple of Poseidon at Paestum had one; all the others had two.[1] Finally, there is the fact that tiles were sometimes pierced with small holes in order to light the room below.[2]

What are we to deduce from this? First, we may dispose of the theory occasionally mooted that the attic was visited only for maintenance. If this were the only reason for visiting the attic, there would be no need for two stone stairways. One would be ample, and in smaller buildings all that would be needed would be a ladder and a movable section of the ceiling; yet we find two stone staircases in buildings such as the Temple of Asclepios at Agrigento, or A Selinus, which had a cella not much wider than a treasury. This shows that in these buildings at least the attic was actually used for something. We have already come to the same conclusion in our study of the Temple of Concord (p. 29). Moreover, the discovery on many sites of pierced tiles (pp. 72 f.) points in the same direction. If the attic were entered only for periodical inspections then lamplight would be quite enough.[3]

The possible uses remaining are as some kind of shrine and for storage. There seems to be evidence for both these theories. Most of the evidence for the shrine has already been set forth in connection with the Temple of Concord (p. 30). For the storage theory we may quote the Temple of Asclepios, Agrigento, where there was probably no room to stand upright in the attic (p. 6, n. 2); the various temples where pierced tiles, showing that the attic was not entered only for maintenance, are not accompanied by stone stairways, showing that some form of wooden ladder was in use;[4] and the fact that in many large mainland temples, notably the Parthenon, where the attic space must have been very large and suited to ceremonial use, there is no evidence at all of stairs leading to it; and the Temple of Poseidon at Paestum, which had only one stairway instead of two.[5]

From this confused and contradictory tangle of evidence—if it can even be dignified by that title—nothing certain can be inferred.[6] We may, however, guess that in some buildings at least the attic was used, and the most probable use seems to have been some combination of shrine and store. I would suggest that the attic may have been used in something the same way as is the apotheke of a museum. Few of the restorations of the interior of a temple give an adequate idea of the great mass of costly offerings that must have left the building somewhat cluttered up.[1] A number of these—possibly the more precious, possibly the more private—would be kept in the attic and shown only to privileged visitors. Such a chamber, half storeroom and half showroom, could well be the explanation of the inconsistencies in the evidence, for the balance between ceremony and utility would vary from one temple to another. This is probably as far as we can safely go in view of the flimsiness of the evidence, but we may deduce from it that in most buildings, where the attic was either inaccessible (except for inspection of the roof) or used mainly for storage, there would be no objection to an encumbering roof structure.[2] In those where the attic partook of the characteristics of the shrine rather than the store, however, a more straightforward system might be preferred, as I have restored at Agrigento.

We must now face up to that perennial problem of Greek roofing, when and where was prop-and-lintel succeeded by the truss? This is a point on which few scholars have cared to tie themselves down to anything definite. The first building where we know for completely certain fact that a truss was used is apparently the Pantheon at Rome, but it is plain that the principle must have been known long before then. There is a tendency to assign its inception to the Hellenistic era. Marquand[3] remarks that 'trussed frames were possibly known to the Greeks but they can hardly have come into use generally except with the steeper-pitched roofs of the Romans'. Dinsmoor[4] believes the truss to have been discovered 'by the Hellenistic period', but later than 330, because the Arsenal of Philo was built without it. P & C, p. 534, ascribe the invention to 'les architectes contemporains d'Empédocle', from a conviction that certain of the wide Sicilian cellas, lacking an interior colonnade, could be covered in no other way.

This last is indeed part of a dilemma very difficult to resolve. Table 1 shows the approximate spans of the cellas of the most important buildings of our period in Greece and Magna Graecia. It will immediately be noted how buildings in Magna Graecia or Sicily, although as large as, or larger than, their counterparts in Greece, nevertheless dispensed with the interior colonnade.[5] There is one important inference to be drawn from this table. The Sicilians felt much more confident in their powers than the Greeks. It is perfectly true that the Greeks could face wide spans; the Parthenon proves that; but the object of the table is not to show how wide a cella the Greeks could span; it shows how such a span was tackled. One thing is clear: when the Greeks had to roof a cella wider than 6·5 m. they broke the span

TABLE I. CELLA SPANS

The figures give the width of the cella from wall to wall; the actual span to be bridged is often less owing to the presence of an internal colonnade. Where this is so it is marked thus: x in the relevant column, followed by figures in parentheses giving the actual clear span between the colonnades. Measurements are in metres.

Magna Graecia and Sicily

Temple	Width	Int. Col.	Source
Basilica, Paestum	11·44	x (5·6)	K & P, pl. II
Ceres, Paestum	5·70	—	K & P, pl. III
Poseidon, Paestum	10·85	x (5·9)	K & P, pl. IV
Tav. Pal., Metaponto	5·60	—	K & P, pl. V
Apollo, Syracuse	9·70	x (3·6)	MA, 1951, p. 815
Athene, Syracuse	9·82	—	K & P, pl. IX
Megaron, Gaggera	8·47	—	K & P, pl. XI
C Selinus	8·50	—	K & P, pl. XII
D Selinus	8·20	—	K & P, pl. XIII
A Selinus	7·50	—	K & P, pl. XV
F Selinus	7·12	—	K & P, pl. XVI
G Selinus	17·93	x (7·15)	K & P, pl. XVII
E Selinus	11·70	—	K & P, pl. XVIII
Heracles, Agrigento	11·84	—	K & P, pl. XXI
Olympieion, Agrigento	12·85	—	K & P, pl. XXIII
Hera, Agrigento	7·68	—	K & P, pl. XXIV
S. Biagio, Agrigento	10·35	—	K & P, pl. XX
Concord, Agrigento	7·55	—	K & P, pl. XXV
Hera, Foce del Sele	6·14	—	Zancani, pl. X
Treasury, Foce del Sele	7·30	—	Zancani, pl. II
Treasury of Gela, Olympia	9·68	—	Kunze & Schlieff, fig. 22

Greece

Temple	Width	Int. Col.	Source
Parthenon	19·20	x (11·05)	Penrose, pl. IV
Theseion	6·24	x (4·74)	Koch, pl. XLI, *Hesp.*, pl. IX, fig. 34
Erechtheion	9·80	—	P & S, pl. II
Sounion	6·53	—	*AM*, 1884, pl. XV
Rhamnous	5·17	—	Gandy
Aphaia	6·28	x (3·85)	*Aegina*, pl. XXXII
Poseidon, Isthmia	11·7	x (c. 7·0)	*Hesp.* 1955, pl. 43c
Tegea	8·94	—	Dugas, pl. IX–XI
Fourth-century Apollo, Delphi	10·72	x (7·32)	F de D, II, pl. IV
Artemis, Kalydon	6·14	x (?)	Dyggve, pp. XXIX, XXXIV
Apollo, Delos	5·70	—	F de Dél, XII, pl. IV
Athenians, Delos	8·34	—	F de Dél, XII, pl. XII
Apollo, Corinth	8·47	x (3·45)	*AJA*, 1905, pl. III
Asclepios, Epidauros	3·95	—	Kavaddias, pl. VI
Zeus, Olympia	13·26	x (8·52)	Olympia, pl. IX
Hera, Olympia	8·37	x (4·84)	Olympia, pl. XVIII
Bouleuterion (S), Olympia	11·07	x (5·53)	Olympia, pl. LV
Bouleuterion (N), Olympia	10·80	x (5·40)	Olympia, pl. LV
Metroon, Olympia	5·08	—	Olympia, pl. XXIV
Bassae	6·81	x (5·23)	Donaldson, pl. II
Artemis, Corcyra	7·37	x (4·1)	Rodenwaldt, pl. I, p. 39
Kardaki, Corcyra	c. 6·0	—	—

up by the insertion of a colonnade;[1] the Sicilians did not. There is no reason why the Sicilians should not have used the inside colonnade. They must have known about it and I cannot believe that it was omitted solely for aesthetic reasons.[2] The West Greeks were highly imitative in all their Doric buildings. There were, it is true, many local traits, but it seems incredible that they should leave out so important a unit on aesthetic grounds alone. It must have been done for structural reasons. They felt that they did not need it. This can only mean that the Sicilians knew of some easy way of spanning a cella and the Greeks did not.

This is a point of such importance that we may repeat the evidence on which it is based. It must be emphasized that the actual size of the cella is not important. The Sicilian cellas were, on the average, larger than the Greek, but not enough to prove anything; and the 11·05 m. span over the central aisle of the Parthenon shows that prop-and-lintel could cope with a big span when it had to.[3] The point is that when faced with any cella other than the smallest the Greeks preferred to break the span up, thus making impossible spans possible and easy spans easier; and the Sicilians did not think it worth while. In short, Table 1 shows that the Greeks found it less trouble to build an inside colonnade than to cross the cella in a clear span, and the Sicilians found it less trouble to cross the cella in a clear span than to build a colonnade. There can be no doubt where this evidence is pointing: the only logical conclusion to draw from it, disregarding everything except the table, is that the Greeks never used the truss in our period, while the Sicilians did, from very early times.[4]

The only other possible explanation is that the Sicilians used lintel-and-prop but were somehow able to make their crossbeams much stronger than the Greeks. This could only be because they had access to better timbers, which were either of larger size or stronger wood. If so, however, it seems impossible that the mainland Greeks would not also have had access to them. We know that they sometimes imported their timbers from some distance away,[5] and had better timber been available in Sicily there is no reason why it should not have been used in Greece too.

The next point to consider is the size of the beams used by the Sicilians. It is impossible to get the size of the crossbeams spanning the cella except in a non-peripteral building. There are two of these on our list; both are very early, and both preserve in their side cornice blocks the cuttings for the crossbeams. The Megaron of Demeter has already been dealt with (p. 24), and we have seen how the internal evidence suggests a truss. The other is that monumentally puzzling building, the

Treasury of Gela at Olympia. This has a very wide span (9·68 m.),[1] and though the arrangement of the beam sockets is most confusing (see Pl. X*a*, *b*) one thing is abundantly clear. There are upwards of thirty cuttings to be found in the side cornice blocks.[2] Most are slightly sloped so as to take the ends of the rafters, but some are cut with level bottoms so that they could have taken the ends of crossbeams. It is often hard to tell which is which, but this at least they have in common: there is no cutting of either sort larger than 28 cm. square. The ridge beam, 37 cm. wide by 32 cm. high, could hardly have spanned a cella of 11·58 m. without aid. The only thing that could have propped it is some cross-structure; and a crossbeam 28 cm. square seems rather light for lintel-and-prop over a 9·68 m. span.[3] It seems to me highly likely that this building was roofed with some sort of a truss, which would permit the use of slighter timbers. This again may appear an unexpected conclusion, but we must remember a fact often overlooked: the Treasury of Gela had one of the widest spans in all Greek classical roofing, being surpassed only by the span over the centre of the cella of the Parthenon.[4]

This does but confirm the conclusions drawn from the table, and we are forced to admit that whatever the outside evidence, the direct evidence of the buildings themselves points logically and inexorably to only one conclusion: the Sicilian architect was acquainted with the principle of the truss, and employed it regularly from about 550 onwards.

The objections to this view are obvious. The chief one is that Sicilian architecture is so imitative and backward relative to that of the mainland that it seems incredible that it could invent for itself a principle so complex; and knowledge of the truss was certainly not, at that date, derived from Greece. This is the dilemma that has tormented many scholars: how could the Sicilians know about the truss if the Greeks did not?

Having taken the decisive step and declared that the Sicilians did in fact know about the truss, we must now seek to discover how they knew. They did not learn about it from the Greeks. Given their uninventive nature, it is unlikely that they thought of it for themselves. This does not exhaust all possibilities; there are still two sources whence the Sicilian architect could possibly have learned of it. One is the Etruscans. This is most unlikely. There is nothing to suggest that the Etruscans knew anything about the truss themselves (see p. 59), and if they did, we would expect to find it influencing the Greek buildings at Paestum rather than those in Sicily. They, however, seem to have been spanned by prop-and-lintel.

But there was another great alien power with its own style of architecture and in close contact with the cities of Sicily—Carthage. We know that in the sixth century there were Carthaginian colonies in Sicily. These would be in close contact with their Hellenic neighbours, and, trusses apart, we would expect them to have some influence on them.

It is unfortunate that we know practically nothing of Carthaginian architecture. We may remember, however, that as a great seapower they would be well acquainted with the truss-like frames used in shipbuilding; and also that we know so little of their architecture and its influence on the Greeks that we cannot rule Carthage out as at any rate a possible source of the truss—I do not claim it as anything more.[1] If this hypothesis is correct, then all our questions are satisfactorily answered. It is quite possible that though in common use in Sicily such a structure should not be adopted in Greece.[2] The first attempts at trusses would in all probability be only partly successful, for even if the design had been fully worked out by Carthage it might well take the Sicilians some time to grasp the principle properly, and acquaintance with these early and unsatisfactory Sicilian trusses might have turned the Greek architects against the idea. We may even be able to quote an actual example of this.

The Treasury of Gela, as we have seen, was probably roofed with a truss; certainly it had a quite exceptionally wide span. At the same time it is likely that in so early a building the truss may not have been fully developed or correctly employed. Moreover, we know for a fact the roof was rebuilt on one or more occasions. May we not hazard a guess that the architect overreached himself and tried to cover a very wide span with an imperfect truss, and that as a result the roof collapsed? This would explain the rebuilding, and so public a demonstration of the frailties of the truss could go far to make it suspect in the eyes of the Greek architect.

Certainly it has often happened in the history of technology of every kind that the general adoption of a new device, destined in the long run to revolutionize technique, has been long delayed by prejudice aroused by the first unsatisfactory prototypes. This might to some extent account for the Greeks' reluctance to copy the early Sicilian trusses, the principles of which they must have found very difficult to understand.[3]

For all these reasons I think that the Sicilians probably knew about the truss, and possibly knew about it from the Carthaginians. It is in fact possible that the truss eventually reached Athens via Sicily and Rome. But there remains one important point to be considered, which is illustrated by Fig. 10. The tie-beams forming the lower member of a row of trusses are tied to the roof timbers and can come at only one level (*a*). Prop-and-lintel construction is not tied in this way, for by using a longer or shorter prop the architect is able to put the crossbeam at any level (*b*). We would therefore expect in a Sicilian trussed building a high cella ceiling. This could be laid on the truss cross members, leaving an unencumbered if somewhat low

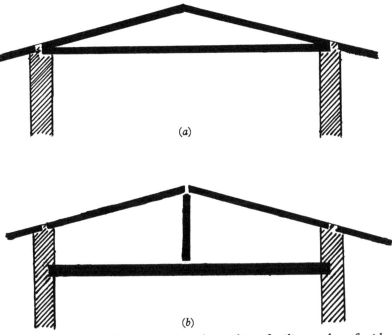

Fig. 10. Diagram illustrating the relationship of ceiling and roof with (*a*) a truss, and (*b*) prop-and-lintel.

attic space above it. But the Temple of Concord has instead a somewhat low cella ceiling, so that if the cella is to be spanned by a truss there will have to be two layers of crossbeams, one carrying the floor of the attic and ceiling of the cella, the other, a metre or so higher, being the cross members of the trusses. This is out of the question, for, apart from the wastefulness of the two layers of crossbeams, they would also obstruct the attic hopelessly. A truss, therefore, seems impossible for this temple, and this is a heavy blow for my theory. Unfortunately, we can follow the same course of reasoning for no other large Sicilian temple, for, most of them having been inadequately studied, in none of the others is the level of the cella ceiling reliably fixed. There is always the chance that Concord had, as I believe it did, a rather more ornamental attic than was usual. If so, the ceiling might have been sunk to give proper headroom, and prop-and-lintel used instead of trusses on account of the low ceiling level. This would be one of the places where an architect, even if he did know about trusses, might prefer prop-and-lintel on account of its making possible a lower ceiling.

This is one of the strongest arguments against the theory that the Sicilians used the truss—the fact that except in very large buildings (but the Sicilians' temples were very large) the truss makes impossible a roomy attic over the cella; and, as we have seen, it would appear from the use of two stone stairways that they attached some importance to this.

Our knowledge of lintel-and-prop construction comes mainly from IG^2, II, 1668, the specification for the Arsenal of Philo. This building was peculiar in that it had no ceiling. The inside colonnade supported the purlins directly, and the crossbeams were laid across at purlin level,[1] thus requiring only a block instead of a prop between themselves and the ridge beam. This structure is very close indeed to being a truss in fact if not in intention, for the intention is that the weight of the ridge beam shall be carried by the crossbeams in prop-and-lintel fashion. The fact that the crossbeam here acts, or could act if the right form of join was used, as a tie between the two purlins is interesting. A similar technique has been suggested for the Temple of Poseidon at Paestum (Fig. 2, between pp. 4 and 5), and, conjecturally, in the Athenian Treasury at Delphi (*RD*, p. 209).

VI

THE PRIMARY TIMBERS

Above the various cross structures discussed in the last chapter came the members that I have designated the primary timbers, that is, the ridge beam and purlins. Of these the ridge beam was a must. I have yet to meet with any evidence suggesting that it could be omitted.[1] The purlins I interpret as substitutes for the cella walls. They broke up the span from ridge to side cornice when it was too long for a rafter to cross unaided. The effect of purlins and ridge beam combined was to break up the whole temple, in plan, into four long, narrow compartments, each of which was narrow enough to be bridged by the rafters in a clear span.

It is usual to find the purlins aligned on the cella walls, but since they are usually narrower than the wall they may not be aligned on the centre of it.[2] I know of only one example of purlins being provided in a non-peripteral building,[3] the Athenian Treasury at Delphi. This might seem an argument against the equation of purlins to cella walls, but in fact it is not, for the woodwork of the Athenian Treasury, whether my restoration of it in *RD* be accepted or not, was peculiar. We should expect it to be roofed with a substantial ridge beam, as treasuries usually were; instead we find ridge beam and purlins, and both remarkably small. This really does look like the woodwork of a large temple scaled down, a conclusion to which I was led independently by my studies of the other timbers of the building (*RD*, p. 212). At all events, the treasury cannot safely be used as a base for deductions on the normal forms of Greek architecture.

In size, both purlins and ridge beams were very substantial timbers, as we may see from the cuttings left for them in the pediments.[4] If anything, the ridge beam is slightly larger. The dimensions of all ridge beam and purlin sockets preserved, with the exception of those in Gaggera roofs, are set down in Table 2. Several points should be noted.

The most peculiar set of primary timbers is that of the Temple of Ceres at Paestum. To begin with, they are exceedingly small. Moreover, the ridge beam is abnormally high; the socket is contained completely within the raking cornice apex block,

TABLE 2

Note. Of sockets marked 'incomplete' only that part contained in the tympanum blocks is preserved, the raking cornice having disappeared, and measurements are of the part remaining. Heights of ridge beam sockets are measured at one side and do not include the sloping top. Purlins are measured on the higher side. Distances recessed are taken from the plane of the tympanum blocks, disregarding the overhang of the raking cornice. Measurements are in centimetres.

Ridge beam sockets

Building	Width	Height	Recessed	Open	Closed	Incomplete
Olympia, Treas. of Gela	37	36	25·5	—	—	x
Olympia, Treas. of Megara	25	36	15·8	—	—	x
Olympia, Treas. of Sicyon	31	51	18·3	—	—	x
Delphi, Athenian Treasury	22·5	40	13	x	—	—
Theseion	48·5	44	56	—	x	—
Sounion	48	29	43	—	x	—
Parthenon	—	70?	—	x?	—	—
Pinakotheke	88	84	16·5	—	x	—
Erechtheion, N. Porch	49·5	59	30·5	—	—	x
Stratos	58·5	54·5	46	—	—	x
Kardaki	13	14	11·5	—	—	x
Concord, Agrigento	36	38	24	x	—	—
Paestum, Ceres	24	34	43	x*	—	—
Paestum, Poseidon	67	91	43	x	—	—
Philo's Arsenal	54	42·5	—	—	—	—

Purlin sockets

Building	Width	Height	Recessed	Open	Closed	Incomplete
Delphi, Athenian Treasury	25	37	13	x	—	—
Theseion	39	59	56	—	x	—
Sounion	40	20	33	—	x	—
Parthenon	93	95	42	—	—	x
Stratos	—	51	34	—	—	x
Concord, Agrigento	52	62	30	x	—	—
Paestum, Ceres	30·5	37·5	9	—	x	—
Paestum, Poseidon (inner)	48·5	103	56·5	x	—	—
Paestum, Poseidon (outer)	74·5	86·5	56	x	—	—

* Entire socket contained in raking cornice block, from face of which recessed measurement is taken.

which is quite unparalleled: every other socket has its bottom down on or in the tympanum blocks. This seems to mean that the rafters, instead of resting on top of the ridge beam as usual, were rabbeted into notches cut in the side of it. Even more peculiar are the purlin sockets. They are closed, and the top is horizontal, so that the socket, viewed in elevation, is rectangular. To the best of our knowledge, purlins normally had a sloped top, on which the rafters rested. Lastly, the seating of these purlins is incredibly narrow, for the sockets are recessed only 9 cm. (the ridge beam, on the other hand, is a perfectly normal 43 cm.). I know the reason for none of these peculiarities.

The enormous size of the purlins of the Parthenon is noteworthy. There were six of them, three on each side of the ridge, and all the same size. The same reasoning applies to them as to the outer purlins of the Temple of Poseidon at Paestum (p. 4); their nearness to roof level in proportion to their width shows that the rafters were rabbeted into the purlins instead of lying on top of them. Several of these cuttings are preserved in the west pediment, equally spaced between ridge and cornice. On the east pediment nothing is preserved except part of a cutting through one of the raking cornice blocks near the south-east corner, which seems to be one side of a purlin cutting.[1] The tympanum block below it is modern. The cutting is of interest because it is tilted, that is, its sides (or, to be correct, side) are at right angles to the roof pitch. Are we to infer that the purlins over the east peristyle were tilted, after the fashion of those at Sounion (Fig. 11, p. 49)? They were certainly not so tilted over the west peristyle, for the cuttings there are of the normal type. I have, however, examined the cutting at the east end several times and, though I cannot be absolutely certain, I believe it to be part of the cutting for the purlin nearest the south-east corner. Its position tallies to within 10 cm. with that of its counterpart at the south-west corner.

How far these purlins continued is uncertain. They did not continue over the cella, for they are not in line with the colonnade. Stevens, in collaboration with Mylonas and Trypanis, has proved that irrespective of what the arrangement over the cella actually was, the soundest by the laws of mechanics would have been a purlin on either side of the internal colonnade (but not on the alignment of the pediment sockets), supported by props from the crossbeams, which act as cantilevers. By this means the cella could be roofed without the use of impossibly large timbers, and if prop-and-lintel was employed the system outlined by Stevens would have been the best way of handling it (*Hesp.* 1955, pp. 250 f.);[1] but this is of course no evidence that the Greeks did in fact actually use such a system. The various plans possible are illustrated and discussed by Mylonas in *AE* 1953–4, pp. 208 ff.

The ridge beam of the Pinakotheke is scarcely representative, for it is only about 3·1 m. long, reaching only to the point at which the hip roof began. There it was presumably supported on a prop from one of the ceiling beams. These were fairly heavy over the cella; the cuttings vary but are on the average for a beam 38 cm. wide by 41 cm. high. An especially large one could have been used to carry the prop, or perhaps it was carried on a short cross-piece between two of them, thus spreading the load. The ridge beam socket in the east wall is preserved, telling us the size of the beam, which is very heavy for so short a span; the two sloping beams under the edges of the hip roof, however, had a much longer span and would have to be fairly heavy; no doubt the builder was influenced by this. We may *en passant* notice that the rafters had a very long span, about 7·50 m., this being the largest rafter span that I know of in mainland Greece.[2]

Sounion also has an interesting set of primary timbers. Three sockets, two for purlins and one for the ridge beam, are to be seen (Fig. 11, Pl. VI*b*, *c*). The purlins were tilted. This is not unparalleled, for I believe that it was done over the east peristyle of the Parthenon (above, p. 47), and it was the normal rule with Gaggera roofs (below, pp. 50 ff.); and the masonry leaves no doubts possible (Pl. VI*b*). These purlins would of course run as far as the first crosswall, there to be carried on by the normal, perpendicular-sided type. The ridge beam is of the same width but not nearly as high as in the Theseion. This is peculiar, in view of the close resemblance between the two temples. It also lacks all the complexities of the Theseion.

The ridge beam of the Kardaki temple is also notable for its diminutive proportions. Only that part of the socket that is in the tympanum block is preserved, and the beam was presumably higher than this. The actual measurements seem to have been about 13 cm. wide by 24·5 cm. high. This can be calculated from the raking cornice blocks, which give the rafter level (see Fig. 13).

In general, I imagine that the primary cuttings in the pediment reflect the arrangement over the whole length of the building. This cannot be taken for granted, for we know of some temples where the beams over the cella were differently arranged. Concord, Agrigento, was one of them, as is shown by the stonework. So apparently was the Parthenon. In the Theseion I have had to modify the purlin spacing over the cella (p. 10). At Sounion, too, there was probably some modification, for, quite apart from the tilting, the purlins show the same discrepancy as in the Theseion (Plommer, p. 86).

Even when they do correspond the same beam would not of course run the whole length of the temple. There would be a break over each crosswall; indeed, the two ends of the beams might be in sockets cut one in each side of the crosswall and not touching, as was done in the Temple of Concord.[1] Alternatively, they

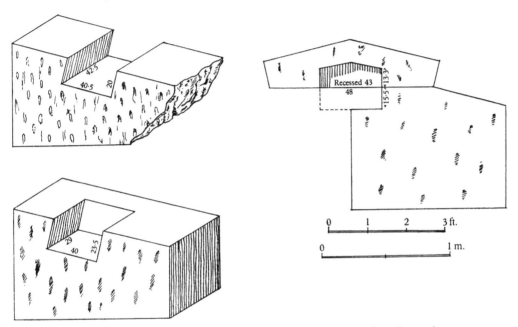

Fig. 11. Temple of Poseidon, Sounion. Ridge beam and purlin sockets.

might be slightly offset so that when they met on top of the crosswall they lay alongside each other in a short overlap, so that they could be bolted together. This was done with the purlins in the Athenian Treasury at Delphi.[2] Over the cella the ridge beam and purlins would be in several sections. This is confirmed by the statement in the Arsenal specification that there was to be a joint over every other column.[3]

The system outlined above, of a ridge beam and two purlins aligned on the cella walls, is that usually restored in temples where nothing is known of the roof structure. It is the traditional form, and for most buildings it is correct. There was, however, a sizeable minority that used a different system, at least over the pronaos and end peristyles.

I first became acquainted with this system in the Megaron of Demeter at Gaggera, and, since this became the key enabling me to understand cuttings in many other buildings that had previously puzzled me, I have named this structure a Gaggera roof. Its dominant characteristic, as demonstrated at Gaggera, is a multitude of small, tilted purlins, replacing the few large ones of normal buildings. They are tilted because this system is suited for use over short spans, so that they did not need to be supported from below. A tilted purlin combines well with the sloping rafters on top, and is the natural form for a member to be laid between two pediments; an ordinary purlin has to be set perpendicularly because it would tend otherwise to slip off the props below it.

The evidence for the Gaggera roof is widespread, but it all takes the same form, namely a block from pediment or crosswall carrying one or more cuttings for small tilted purlins. When we find such a block we may be reasonably sure that we are dealing with a Gaggera roof. Such blocks are to be found in eleven buildings. These are enumerated in Table 3, p. 53, and certain of them are illustrated in Fig. 12. The similarity of most of the blocks in this plate to blocks *a* or *b* in Fig. 7 is too marked to require comment, but a few remarks may not be out of place. One important difference should be grasped, the distinction between high and low siting. These cuttings are made in either the tympanum blocks or the raking cornice. Gaggera has shown that the tiles could be laid direct on the purlins; this is possible only if they are set very high, right up under the tiles; therefore the cuttings for a roof of this sort will be found in the raking cornice. If, on the other hand, the cuttings are lower down, in the tympanum blocks, then this is impossible. These low-sited purlins are a source of some difficulty, for it is never[1] possible to match one of them with the cornice block that lay above it, so that we cannot tell how much further up, if at all, the socket was carried. In fact, I imagine that most of them were closed by the cornice block and did not extend into it. Likewise, even when the socket is sited high there may still be room for a thin rafter—with the many close-spaced purlins of a Gaggera roof the rafters did not need to be thick—between beam and tile. Both the Megaron and the Temple of Concord have been already discussed, so we may omit them and pass straight on to the blocks from other buildings.

APHAIA. The evidence is to be found in two raking cornice blocks. One is illustrated in Fig. 12 and in Pl. VII*c*, the other in Pl. VII*b*. The dimensions of the cuttings in

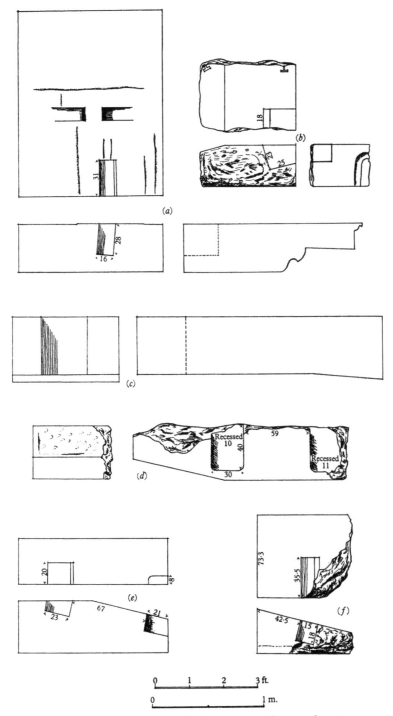

Fig. 12. Blocks from pediment or crosswall that give evidence of a Gaggera roof. (a) and (b) Aphaia; (c) C Selinus; (d) Temple of Zeus, Olympia; (e) Metroon, Olympia; (f) E Selinus.

51

these two blocks are much the same.[1] The depth of the cutting relative to its width would normally lead us to restore a rafter on top of it, so as to leave the beam more or less square. This cannot be, for both cuttings exhibit a peculiarity unique in Greek roofing; instead of the socket's being at right-angles to the roof slope it is slightly tilted (but not nearly enough to make it perpendicular to the building). This is most odd, and there is only one explanation. There was only one part of the whole temple that was set at the angle at which the socket is cut. This was the tiles. Collectively, the tiles follow the roof slope; individually, each is at an angle slightly shallower, as its lower edge is raised by resting on the tile below. This is the angle of the cuttings, and there would be no point in setting them at it unless the beams that they contained were actually in contact with the tiles. I therefore believe that the tiles rested directly on the purlins without the interposition of clay, sheathing, battens, or rafters, the purlins being spaced one under each tile joint.[2] The block in Pl. VIIc carries a slight dressing for the tile, showing that the edge of the tile was approximately over the middle of the purlin. The direction of the tilt shows that the block in Fig. 12 and Pl. VIIc comes from the south-west or north-east cornice, that in Pl. VIIb from the north-west or south-east.

We must also mention the block shown in Fig 12b. This block carries part of a cutting for a tilted, Gaggera-type purlin. As the raking cornice block carries quite a different kind of socket, we are probably to assume that this block comes from one of the crosswalls. The groove for the lifting rope is cut upside down. Presumably after the block had been hoisted up there was some change of plan; it may have been meant for somewhere else and re-cut to its present shape up aloft to save the trouble of raising and lowering. The clamp mark shows which side is really the top.

c SELINUS. The raking cornice blocks published by K & P, fig. 77, are still to be seen, but are too embedded in the earth to be measured. According to K & P they are lying in the order they occupied when *in situ*. If so, the spacing of the purlin sockets that they carry is irregular, which is peculiar but by no means impossible in a building as early and given to irregular woodwork as C Selinus.

It is unlikely that the sockets were continued down into the tympanum blocks; they are quite big enough as it is. Indeed, they are really too large for the purlins of a Gaggera roof, even though it is a big temple. The Temple of Zeus at Olympia was a big building too, but its Gaggera purlins were only 30 × 40 cm. Possibly this is not a Gaggera roof at all, but simply a roof of ordinary tilted purlins, like that over the east peristyle of the Parthenon. If so, K & P's spacing of the blocks, with the cuttings so close together, is to be questioned.[1]

TABLE 3. GAGGERA ROOFS

Dimensions of beams, in centimetres

Building	Width	Height	Interaxial spacing	Siting High	Low	Illustration
Megaron of Demeter:						
Pronaos	11·5	10·5	72·5	—	x*	Fig. 7*b*
Cella	20	23	72·5	—	x*	Fig. 7*a*
Aphaia	16	28	?	x	—	Fig. 12*a*
C Selinus	80	95	—	x	—	Fig. 12*c*
E Selinus	15	18	?	—	x	Fig. 12*f*
Metroon, Olympia	23	13·5	90	—	x	Fig. 12*e*
Zeus, Olympia	30	40	89	x	—	Fig. 12*d*
Concord, Agrigento	38	34	*c.* 89	x	—	Fig. 9
Kardaki, Corcyra	*c.* 23	11	?	x	—	Fig. 13
Artemis, Corcyra	38	23	167	x	—	—
Hera, Agrigento	?	?	?	—	x	—
Crimisa	*c.* 20	22	—	—	x	—

* Cutting in tympanum blocks, but high relative to roof level.

E SELINUS. I do not know for certain from what part of the building comes the stone illustrated in Fig. 12*f* and Pl. VIII*b*, but I think that it is from the top of one of the crosswalls. The cutting is fairly slight, like those in the pronaos of the Megaron of Demeter. We should expect a small beam, such as might support a row of tiles directly, but hardly a layer of rafters as well. We should therefore expect the beam (and the cutting) to be up close in under the roof; which is impossible if the block is from the pediment.

ZEUS, OLYMPIA. The block shown in Fig. 12*d* is part of the raking cornice, from the corner where it meets the horizontal cornice. This is assured by the existence of a companion block still carrying part of the cornice proper and also a tiny part of one of the purlin sockets. The position of this block shows that not only did the temple have a Gaggera roof over the end peristyle, but that instead of being confined to that part of the peristyle between the pronaos antae, as in Concord, Agrigento, it extended the full width of the building. The outermost purlins presumably had their other ends carried on an exceptionally heavy rafter reaching from above the pronaos anta to the side cornice.

METROON, OLYMPIA (Fig. 12e). This block, in yellowish poros, is lying among several frieze blocks of the same material, and is attributed by Kunze to the Metroon (see p. 56, n. 4). The block is shown in Pl. VIIId.

KARDAKI (Fig. 13). Two raking cornice blocks are preserved carrying cuttings for tilted purlins in the lower half of the block. This shows that the top of the purlins was 12·5 cm. below tile level, giving this for the rafter thickness. The cuttings were apparently not continued into the tympanum blocks as they were in the nearby Temple of Artemis (below). Many of the tympanum slabs are still to be seen (Fig. 13, opposite), and none of them carry sockets. It is always possible that there were sockets in those missing, but this would give a very irregular spacing of the beams. It may also be noted that two of the tympanum slabs preserved are those opposite the cella wall, ruling out any possibility that the two sockets preserved belonged to tilted purlins of the normal type (for instance, as at Sounion). If this were so, the purlins would be aligned on the cella wall, and would also be larger than are the existing sockets, so that there would be some kind of cutting in the tympanum slab; and there is none.

ARTEMIS, CORCYRA. I could find none of the relevant blocks and have to rely on Rodenwaldt.[1] He restores a Gaggera roof with very widely spaced purlins. As at Kardaki, the cuttings are closed, 16 cm. below tile level. Unlike Kardaki they are carried down into the tympanum slabs.

HERA, AGRIGENTO. This is doubtful. I include it on the strength of one tympanum block carrying part of one side of a tilted purlin socket, but whether it had a proper Gaggera roof or simply tilted purlins, as at Sounion, I cannot say.

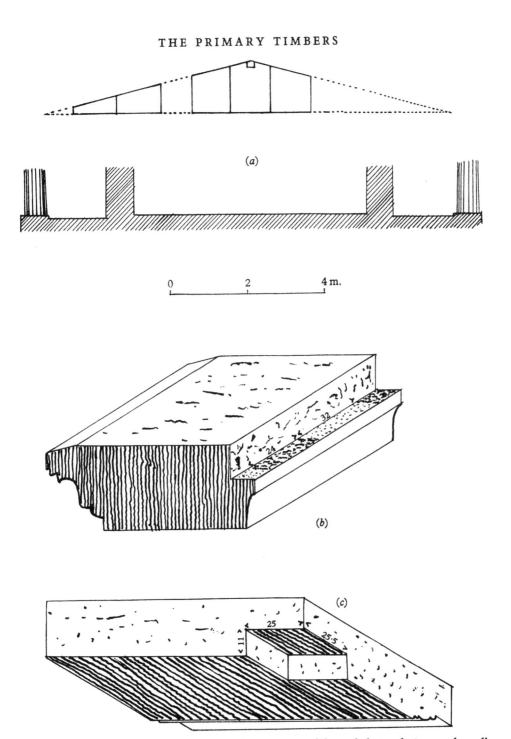

Fig. 13. Temple at Kardaki. (*a*) Preserved tympanum slabs and their relation to the cella wall; (*b*) side cornice block; (*c*) raking cornice block.

CRIMISA. I have not seen this block myself and rely on Orsi's drawing of it.[1] Orsi thinks it is one of a pair of ordinary purlins, but the size of the temple makes it unlikely. The span was about 7·3 m., which is quite large.

This then is the Gaggera roof. The evidence shows that it was widely used, generally over the end peristyle and (probably) pronaos and opisthodomos. It is a form of roofing unsuited to long spans, for the numerous small purlins are very difficult to prop up, unless they rest on a truss. For this reason I imagine that it was not much used over cellas, except possibly in Sicilian buildings, many of which I suspect to have used trusses anyway.[2]

It seems sometimes to have been used for a substitute for the rafters (Gaggera, Aphaia); at others it is quite certain that rafters were laid on top of it (Kardaki, Artemis Corcyra, C Selinus). In other temples the position is less certain, but the rafters must often have been very thin (Zeus Olympia).

One further point of interest may be observed from a comparison of Tables 2 and 3. With two exceptions, both of which seem to have been oddities in their roof construction in any case,[3] all the buildings carrying actual sockets for purlins of the normal type, enumerated in Table 2, are dated later than 460. With two exceptions and one borderline case[4] all those with sockets for Gaggera roofs, as shown in Table 3, are earlier. May we not draw from this a deduction of some importance: that the Gaggera roof was the normal way of roofing the end peristyle and other parts enjoying a short span between two crosswalls throughout the Greek world until about 460, and about then was superseded by what is thought of as the standard form, employing a few large, vertical-sided purlins? No doubt the change-over was gradual. I have suggested (RD, p. 212) that the Athenian Treasury at Delphi reflects the construction of a large building, and this building would seem to have been constructed on post-460 lines.[5] Also, the first temple in which large, standard purlins actually appear is the Temple of Poseidon at Paestum; and with the time-lag in development between Greece and the West this ought to mean that the system was already well established on the mainland. On the other hand, the Gaggera roof, as we have seen at Agrigento, could be used as part of the decoration of the attic, and its life in Sicily may have been prolonged for that reason. We must therefore avoid tying ourselves down to any definite date for the change-over, which was gradual and involved a long overlap.

I can assign no reason to the change other than increasing architectural skill. The normal roof is a more sophisticated system, arguing greater skill in woodwork, greater breadth of vision, and a greater readiness to consider the temple as a whole. The Gaggera roof stands for treating each part of the temple as a separate unit, and roofing it as is most convenient. Its great advantage over the standard system is that it replaces the few large timbers with a number of smaller ones, which would be more easily obtained and transported. Its great disadvantage is that such a roof cannot easily be supported on props from below; it must run as a free span between two pediment-shape crosswalls. It was thus a structure suited for use over the pronaos and end peristyle, but not over the cella. The only exception to this is afforded by buildings spanned by trusses, for the triangular frame of the truss provides a natural resting place for the row of little purlins. We might perhaps therefore expect to find Gaggera roofs and trusses going together, and it is possibly significant that, according to the present interpretation, both appear frequently in Sicily. We must nevertheless remember that with the exception of Gaggera itself we know of no definite example of a Gaggera roof over a cella.

The Gaggera roof had a long history, and we may in conclusion glance at two later examples of it. The first represents the only ancient building where remains of the actual woodwork are preserved, the Casa del Telaio at Herculaneum. This roof was originally published in *AJA*, 1941, p. 469; since then, it has been dealt with in Professor A. Maiuri's book, *Ercolano* (p. 427). On excavation enough charred fragments were found *in situ* to permit a complete restoration of the roofing timbers. Professor Maiuri has very kindly sent me a drawing illustrating the system found, and this I include as Fig. 14. It will be seen how in its adherence to the principle of using a number of small purlins so as to distribute the load it is in the direct tradition of the Gaggera roof.

This tradition did not die with Herculaneum, but lived on to see frequent use in modern construction. A typical example is shown in Pl. VIII*a*. The structure of the building can be clearly seen from the outside. It is spanned by a series of trusses. Resting on these and the end walls is a row of six Gaggera-type purlins. These in turn carry the rafters and battens on which the tiles are laid. Although this form of construction can be seen all through Italy, the building illustrated is perhaps its most fitting representative, for it is to be found only a few hundred yards from the site at Gaggera that proved the key to the problem.

Before leaving the primary timbers we may make a slight digression. It is remarkable how little the structure of the roof in Magna Graecia was affected by the traditional forms of the Etruscans, with whom the Greeks were in close contact. The Etruscan roof differed from the Greek in many ways, but in none more than

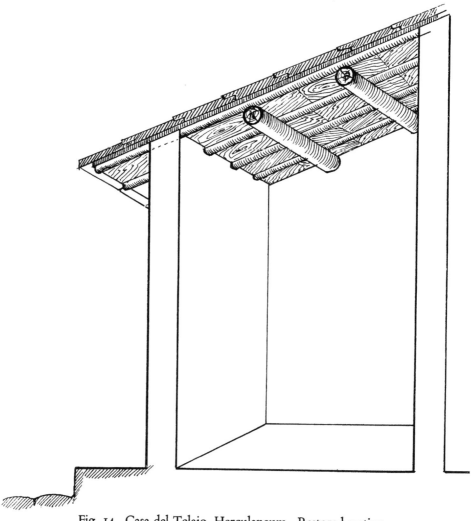

Fig. 14. Casa del Telaio, Herculaneum. Restored section.
(Drawing by Soprintendenza alle Antichità, Naples.)

its emphasis on the ridge beam. In Greek work this tends to be only slightly, if at all, heavier than the purlins; in Gaggera roofs it is often very slight and no bigger than the small purlins.[1] But in Etruscan roofing it is enormous. This may be seen both from models[2] and from the surviving terra-cotta plaques that covered its projecting end.[1] It was made so large for two reasons. First, it had to carry the load of a heavy set of terra-cotta ridge decorations that sometimes even included statues.[2] Second, the ridge beam had to carry the weight of the roof unaided, for the Etruscans apparently did not use purlins, preferring one really big ridge beam. This is proved by their apparent absence from Vitruvius' Etruscan temple, and the fact that they never appear in the numerous temple models.[3]

The ridge beam was supported on vertical props. This is confirmed by the tombs of Cerveteri and Tarquinia, the interiors of which are regularly carved or painted to represent the inside of a house. There the normal treatment of the pediment is a heavy beam across the base, a pier at its mid-point, and, resting on top, the ridge beam. Sometimes this pier is given a rudimentary capital (of the Aeolic or Proto-Ionic type) and base. This shows that the pediment had a prop supporting the ridge beam, and, one presumes, more if required to support the raking cornice beams. We may note in the Doric Temple at Cori, Pl. VII a, how this treatment could become translated into stone in the form of vertical blocks with the intervals filled in with rubble.

This shows that the Etruscans, like the Greeks, did not use the truss, but, in our period at least, relied on prop-and-lintel. Here, however, we must consider the stone lid of a cinerary urn in the Archaeological Museum at Florence. It has not hitherto been published.[4] As so often, the lid was cut into a rough likeness of a house roof. This is very common, but the treatment of the part of the lid corresponding to the gable is unique. It is shown in Pl. VIII c. The top of this lid is cut into the shape of a tiled roof, and it can scarcely be disputed that the lines cut into the side shown are meant to represent the various timbers holding the roof up.

It is abundantly plain that what we are looking at is some kind of truss; moreover, it is not the form most commonly used (which is pictured in Fig. 8 b, bottom). There is, however, another form of truss (Fig. 8 b, middle), which is still in use today in contemporary construction in England, and its resemblance to the Etruscan lid is obvious. Although normally a less efficient form of truss, it has the advantage of being more stable in a building with a low-pitched roof, and so would be especially suited to use in classical architecture. Whether it was the form of truss in use throughout the classical world I cannot say, but the lid seems to prove that it was known. No doubt allowance must be made for artistic inaccuracies in the representation on the lid, but it must remain as a piece of evidence of both interest and importance, for it is the only actual picture known of the truss as used in the ancient world.

VII

THE SECONDARY TIMBERS

Whether a Gaggera roof or the more orthodox form was employed, the disposition of the primary timbers was tied to the design of the building below them, inexorably governed by the spacing of the various walls. On top came the secondary timbers, the lowest and most important being the rafters. These were less affected by the placing of the walls, for the aim and effect of the primaries was to create a single uniform system along the whole length of the building on which the secondaries could be laid without interruption from the various crosswalls. This generalization, it is true, often breaks down for buildings with Gaggera roofs, which no doubt affected the size of rafters laid on them, where they did not replace them altogether, but it holds good for most buildings.

The rafters were tied rather to the tile spacing than to the design of the building below. The weight of a tiled roof was not uniformly distributed but was greatest under the tile joints, owing to the cover tiles and the thickening of the pantiles at the edge. It was but commonsense to space the rafters under each tile joint. That this was done can be seen from the famous Dionysos relief in Naples (Noack, *Baukunst des Altertums*, pl. 61); it can plainly be seen that in the two buildings in the background the ends of square rafters project out under the eaves, centred under the tile joints. This practice is confirmed by many buildings where the sima joints, as shown by the dowels, coincide with the rafter spacing, as shown by the sockets (for example, Bassae,[1] Zeus Nemea (Fig. 20 and Pl. IX*a*), E Selinus).

Although this was the usual rule, it was not universal. In early buildings there seems often to have been a thick layer of sheathing and clay that made a correspondence of rafters and tile joints unnecessary, and in buildings of this type the rafter spacing can be, and is, quite irregular. We see this principle at work in Temple C Selinus, where the upper cornice members, on which the rafters rested, show a succession of cuttings for their lower ends that are scattered broadcast and often overlap (as may be seen from Gabrici's drawings in *MA*, 1929, pl. XIII). The same thing happens in the Treasury of Gela at Olympia (Pl. X*a*, *b*). In both of these buildings the irregularity of the sockets precludes not only any relationship between the rafters and the tile spacing, but apparently even any constant relationship of the rafters to each other. Apparently the principle was that if there was a large timber to hand it was used as it stood without any attempt to trim it down to standard size, and the next one laid a little further away. The actual overlaps in the cuttings were caused by renewals of the roof. Other buildings of course had their roofs renewed too, but where the rafters were on a fixed spacing obviously the replacements would have to go into the old sockets.

At Delphi there are several interesting cornice blocks to be found near the east end of the Temple of Apollo. They are in reddish sandstone and come from one of the treasuries. They are peculiar in that they seem to have been cut to take the ends of a continuous deck of rafters laid side by side with no gaps in between. These were not of a uniform size, but on an average 15 cm. wide and about the same height. Their ends did not all stop on the same line; some projected further than others into the block, which thus bears, as it were, a collective imprint of them all that makes it possible to judge the width of each individual rafter. This effect may be seen in Pl. IX b. With the exception of the conjectural restoration over the attic of the Temple of Concord at Agrigento, this is the only example of a continuous deck of rafters, though they could sometimes be laid very close together (see p. 93).

It is now time to climb up one step further and examine the small but important space between the rafters and the tiles. In doing so we approach another of the perennial problems of archaeology, which may be termed the problem of the battens.

Until the end of the last century it was usual to restore rafters either square in cross-section or rather flattish (relying on the traditional equation of mutules and rafter ends), and then to lay the roof tiles directly on top of them. There was no justification for this other than the belief that in the absence of any evidence to the contrary the simplest solution was also the most likely to be right. Towards the end of the century, however, the evidence to the contrary appeared.

It appeared in the form of two building inscriptions. One was the specification for the construction of a continuous roof along on top of the walls of Athens;[1] the other is the specification for the Arsenal of Philo.[2] These inscriptions prescribed a much more complicated structure, of rafters, battens, sheathing and clay, and their effect on published restorations of other buildings was both immediate and widespread. Henceforth every building was given a roof of this sort, even when it involved serious difficulties.

It was during this period that there appeared the great German publication of *Olympia*, the architectural portions of which were contributed by Doerpfeld.[1] Doerpfeld had already some seven years earlier published a comprehensive study of the Arsenal,[2] so it comes as no great surprise to find every building at Olympia restored with a batten-and-clay roof. We also find it in Fiechter's restoration of the Temple of Aphaia.[3]

The first scholar to adduce any evidence that this might not have been the universal rule seems to have been Wood, who, 'in a paper read before the American School in Athens in 1907 but not yet published',[4] apparently demonstrated that in the Pinakotheke the tiles rested directly on the woodwork without the interposition of a layer of clay.[5]

Twenty years later a further blow was struck against the clay theory with the appearance of the Paton and Stevens publication of the Erechtheion. This building, it appeared, had the tiles laid directly on the battens without either clay or sheathing. The authors were apparently led to this conclusion by three considerations. First, there was the unpublished work of Wood. Second, there is no mention of clay or sheathing in the building inscriptions, otherwise very full and explicit. Third, as they pertinently remarked, 'the use of such a layer of clay was probably general in Greece on buildings which had terracotta tiles. There is, however, no evidence of its use in connection with marble tiles.'

This view, that terra-cotta tiles rested on clay, sheathing, battens and rafters, and marble tiles on battens and rafters alone, is perhaps the view most widely held today.[6]

Nevertheless, there seems to be a certain feeling that these complicated structures are at the best but a regrettable necessity, and a desire to return, where possible, to the simplicity of Cockerell's day. No one, so far as I know, has publicly advocated the jettisoning of the clay and battens restored in so many buildings in obedience to the dictates of the two inscriptions, but it is not too uncommon to come across a drawing in which the tiles lie directly on the rafters and then find no reference in the text to this phenomenon.[7]

For each of these structures there is something to be said. We will find it most convenient to consider five different systems, representing all the combinations of

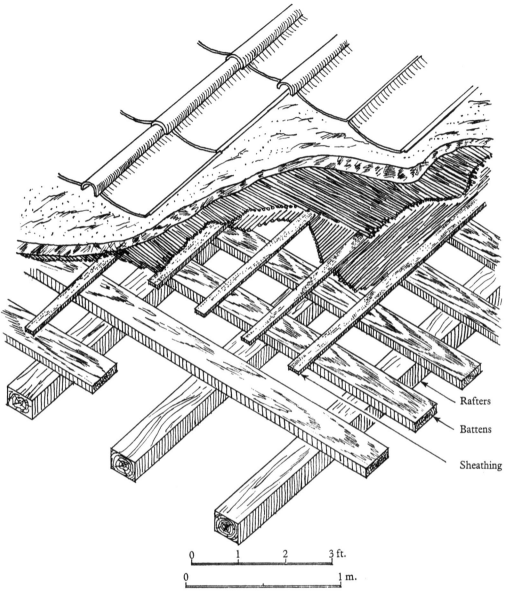

Fig. 15. Roof of gallery on the walls of Athens.
(After Caskey, *AJA*, 1910.)

the secondary timbers possible. First, the tile could be laid in a bed of clay; under this would come sheathing, battens, and rafters (see Fig. 15). Second, the tiles might be laid directly on the sheathing without the clay layer. Third, they could lie on the battens. Fourth, we can omit everything except the rafters. Fifth, and finally, we can omit even the rafters and lay the tiles on the purlins of a Gaggera roof. There is evidence of varying weight supporting all these hypotheses.

Of especial interest is the parallel of modern construction. On a great many buildings in both Greece and Italy the tiles are still of a pattern very similar to that used in ancient times, differing only in being smaller. There is in frequent use a flat tile so constructed as to interlock with its neighbours and make a cover tile unnecessary (cf. the tiles of Bassae); there is the ordinary Corinthian pantile with the joint covered by a semicircular cover tile;[1] lastly, there is the curved pantile and curved cover tile.[2] The systems of woodwork provided to hold these tiles vary greatly. They can be laid directly on the rafters. This is not too common, but it can be done, as is shown by Pl. IX d. This is part of the modern roof built over the Casa dei Vetii at Pompeii. The pantiles are flat and reasonably large, so that it must be quite a close parallel to an ancient roof. A similar modern roof in the Villa dei Misterii shows that such construction can deal quite easily with a large span. There the span is 4·70 m.: the pantiles are about 46 × 30 cm., and the rafters about 12 cm. high by 8 cm. wide. Among other things, this certainly shows how excessively large were the timbers that the Greeks used.

Pl. XI b shows another modern roof in the Casa dei Vetii. This time the tiles are of the smaller, interlocking type, and are laid on a row of Gaggera purlins, with no rafters. This again is not very common. It is more usual to have fewer purlins and some kind of light rafters. Apart from these three simple schemes there are also in use more elaborate structures. First, the tiles can be laid on the battens. Second, sheathing can be laid to form a continuous deck, and the tiles laid on this. Alternatively, the sheathing boards can be laid with intervals left open between them (which is a very close parallel to the construction prescribed for the Gallery on the Walls), and the tiles laid on this. This is the structure of the roof of the British School at Athens (see Pl. IX c). It is laid with curved Laconian-type tiles. Plaster is laid in long strips under the ridge and cover tiles to ensure a good watertight join. It is also used in a thick bed at the eaves to stop up the chinks over and under the curved surfaces of the tiles, and to cement the join between the roof and the wall. This is standard practice in modern Greek building, except when the interlocking type of tile is used. I have never seen, in Greece or Italy, a roof in which the tiles were laid in a continuous layer of plaster or clay. It will be seen that these modern systems have certain affinities with ancient construction, and this will become more apparent as we proceed to examine in turn each one of the five forms of ancient construction possible.

I. TILES, CLAY, SHEATHING, BATTENS, RAFTERS, PURLINS. The evidence in favour of this arrangement is to be found in the two inscriptions already mentioned, that for the Gallery on the Walls (*IG*², I, 463) and that for the Arsenal (*IG*², II, 1668). According to the latter there are to be rafters (σφηκίσκοι), battens (ἱμάντες), and sheathing (καλύμματα). Then, δορώσας, the contractor is to lay the tiles. The relevant portion of the Gallery inscription is much longer and much less precise, but the system described is more or less the same as that of the Arsenal. However, not one of the various members is called by the same name. The rafters are now δοκίδες, the battens ἐπιβλῆτες, the sheathing ἱμάντες. Moreover, the clay is to be mixed with straw and laid on a bed of rushes.

This confusion in terms has extended also to the modern commentators, and in the absence of a defined terminology the battens can be referred to by a multiplicity of terms—battens, cross-battens, cross-cleats, cross-laths, slats, furring strips, and many others. To avoid any such ambiguities as involved the ancient writers and threaten to involve the modern, I have restored the Gallery roof according to Caskey's interpretation, and marked on it the parts to which I apply the various terms (Fig. 15).

The presence of a clay layer in these two buildings is certain, but about its disposition I cannot feel so confident. Hitherto it has always been assumed that the clay was to be laid in a continuous bed. This could be right, and must be borne in mind along with the following remarks, but I cannot be sure. There seems no doubt that such a technique was in use, for I have been assured that tiles have been found in Chios bearing traces of mud still adhering to their underside that was of a texture and consistency quite different from that from which they were excavated; and it is quite probable that some of the larger Laconian tiles did lie in a bed of clay to support them firmly, since even those in everyday non-monumental use were $1\frac{1}{2}$ ft. wide, and only 2 cm. thick.[1] Therefore I believe that some buildings had a clay layer, but there are none that I can fix on with certainty.

The Arsenal and the Gallery seem at first obvious candidates, but after a closer inspection of the inscriptions one is less certain. That clay was used in the construction of the roof is indisputable; its disposition is, however, described mainly by that enigmatic verb, δορόω. This word occurs only three times with certainty, twice in the Gallery inscription and once in the Arsenal; in addition there is a doubtful reference at Delos, and one occurrence of the noun δόρωσις (see Appendix III, p. 125). This is all that is known of the word; its derivation is uncertain.

One point leaps to the eye. Its use in the Arsenal is such that it must be not a general word but a technical term, and one describing a whole process. There the whole operation of laying the clay is referred to summarily by the one word δορώσας. Now the wording of this inscription is in all other respects extremely precise, and it is plain that by this one word, it was thought, any competent builder would know exactly what to do. This is discouraging, for anyone with inside knowledge of a trade will know that it is often quite impossible for an outsider to guess the meaning of many of the trade terms, by derivation or otherwise. There is, therefore, little to be gained from pondering over the possible antecedents of the word, and we must turn our attention to the passages where it occurs in the Gallery inscription.

This is much longer, and, in spite of a specious air of accuracy, much vaguer, than the Arsenal inscription (as is demonstrated by the variety of reconstructions made using it as a basis). Indeed, it bears all the signs of being the work of not one man but a committee, with various clauses added piecemeal to satisfy the demands and objections of the different members. As a guide to the meaning of δορόω it is disappointing. We might perhaps guess that it means something like 'building up' or 'laying a layer'; also, when applied to roofing it involves laying rushes 'over and under' (whatever that may mean); and the whole operation is to leave a stratum of clay 'three fingers thick'. This is very little to go on, and there is little reason to assume that the clay must have been laid in a thick, continuous layer in preference to any other arrangement that might be found possible.

We may turn here for a moment to another proviso of the specification. Both cover and ridge tiles were 'all to be laid in clay' (τιθεὶς τοὺς καλυπτῆρας ὅλους ἐν πηλῶι, l. 71). Of this exceedingly clear statement Caskey makes no mention in his text, and in his reconstruction (Fig. 15) the cover tiles are not in contact with the clay at all. Yet the meaning is clear: strips of clay are to be laid under the ridge and cover tiles to ensure a good joint, exactly as in modern work.[1]

Since modern roofs then parallel the Gallery inscription in every respect except the clay layer, we may perhaps wonder if this is correct; and whether it is at all possible that by δορόω was meant the practice of packing clay under and over the curved surfaces of the tiles at the eaves, so as to stop up all the crannies. True, the eaves were protected by a γεῖσον, but the clay and rushes could be added to ensure a watertight join, as was done under ridge and cover tiles. The packing at the eaves, meant to unify the roof tiles and the γεῖσον, would not extend very far back, and the roof would then become an openwork structure of sheathing and battens 'three palms apart', with the Laconian tiles laid on top. The tiles were probably 1½ ft. square at least, and would rest on this structure if anything rather more satisfactorily than would rushes and clay, which might have tended, bit by bit, to fall through the holes. This is indeed another objection to the conventional interpretation. Certainly, nobody asked to restore a framework suitable for the support of a layer of clay would ever have thought of drawing a criss-cross of woodwork that left open a series of large, square holes, and it may be noted that though scholars have restored a roof involving a layer of clay in many buildings, no one has ever dared to reproduce the open woodwork of the Gallery inscription under it. It is perfectly true that a clay layer is more to be expected with Laconian tiles than with Corinthian, but we are hampered by the fact that the Gallery is the only Laconian-roofed building in which we know anything at all about the roofing woodwork. Certainly I cannot understand why the flat Corinthian tiles that covered the Arsenal should have been laid in a continuous bed of clay.

Whether this hypothesis is correct or not I cannot say, but I feel that it is a possibility to be borne in mind, especially as, as we shall see, the clay layer was in fact quite unnecessary.

2. TILES, SHEATHING, BATTENS, RAFTERS, PURLINS. There is no positive evidence in ancient Greek work for such a system. The most definite point is that since curved Laconian tiles might not have lain too well on a basis of battens alone,[1] sheathing might have had to be provided. Sheathing was sometimes also provided for flat tiles, as is shown by its presence in the Arsenal (l. 58). I can see no reason why these should not have been laid often direct on the sheathing, without a clay layer. Terra-cotta tiles are extremely tough and normally can be broken only by some severe shock, such as being dropped on a stone floor. Since they would be under no stress at all when in position, they should not have required clay to support them. Nor would they require it to hold them in place, for the slope of the modern roof is much the same as the ancient, and modern tiles are almost invariably held in place

by gravity alone; being smaller, they do not even have, as a rule, the interlocking notches that helped the ancient tiles to hold their position.

Moreover, if a clay layer was largely unnecessary, it can also be shown to have been impractical in many buildings. We have already seen how the space available for the secondary timbers in the Temple of Poseidon at Paestum (p. 8) was very limited. If we have to allow space for sheathing and clay[1] as well as for battens, then the rafters cannot have been much more than 17 cm. thick, which is impossibly little when it is remembered that the addition of the clay will double, if not treble, the weight of the roof. It seems often to have been overlooked that the provision of a clay layer not only makes the rafters thinner, but at the same time increases the load on them, so that the strain on the rafter is multiplied anything up to five or six times.

I therefore believe that in many buildings the tiles were laid direct on the sheathing, if indeed even that member was provided. At the same time we must recognize that certain early buildings must have had at least sheathing, if not clay as well. They are those already mentioned (pp. 60 f.) where the rafter spacing is irregular.

Of these the classic example is the Treasury of Gela at Olympia. The variety of size and shape of rafter cutting displayed by the side cornice blocks is both astonishing and baffling. Kunze and Schlieff[2] claim to identify two separate series of cuttings superimposed, one large and one small. The three blocks shown in Pl. X*a* lend colour to this idea, but this logical progression seems to break down when we look at the other blocks. There are a considerable number of these lying around the site, and Pl. X*b* shows these viewed, as it were, from the ridge of the building. The wide, not to say wild, variety of cutting needs no comment. The stones were at one stage in their history built into a Byzantine wall, but none of these cuttings can be blamed on the Byzantine masons. It is plain that the roof consisted of irregular timbers set on an irregular spacing, and therefore there must at least have been battens, and almost certainly sheathing as well, so as to reduce the irregularities of the rafters to a smooth, unbroken deck on which the tiles could easily be laid. I must confess that I can see no systematic spacing in the cuttings—what are we to make of a block where three large cuttings come so close together that they run into each other? In particular, I am utterly defeated by the block shown in Fig. 16 and Pl. XI*e*.

3. TILES, BATTENS, RAFTERS, PURLINS. It can be proved beyond doubt that tiles were laid directly on the battens, the two most important pieces of evidence being

offered by the Erechtheion and the Pinakotheke. In both the Pinakotheke and the south-west wing of the Propylaia the roof left a sloping groove carved where it abutted on the east wall. The upper surface of this groove is carved roughly into a series of steps to accommodate the tiles; the floor of the groove is left plain in the south-west wing, but in the Pinakotheke it carries a series of slight recesses, becoming deeper as the roof rises, to accommodate the ends of the battens. This groove is shown in Pl. XI*a*. From these cuttings it becomes clear that the battens were set not on the pitch of the roof, but on that of the individual tiles, which, of course, lay at a slightly shallower angle. It is at this shallower angle that the cuttings were made,

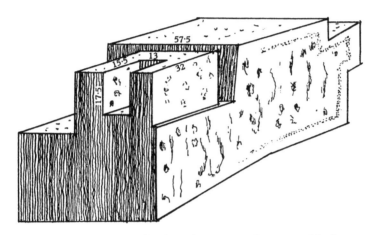

Fig. 16. Treasury of Gela, Olympia. Side cornice block.

and the inference is obvious: the battens were in contact with the tiles. This fact has not to my knowledge been published, but presumably formed the basis of the paper by Wood referred to by P & S (p. 369).

The evidence of the Erechtheion is largely negative, but convincing. It is to be found in the fact that the building inscriptions dealing with the roof refer to rafters (σφηκίσκοι) and battens (ἱμάντες) (for example, P & S, pp. 340, 368), but never to sheathing.[1] From this P & S deduce that the tiles lay directly on the battens, without any sheathing or clay. It is to be noted that they restore two battens under each tile joint in parts of the building.

The only other building showing actual traces of battens is the Temple of Poseidon at Paestum, if I have rightly interpreted the meaning of the depression along the raking cornice, but, as we have already noted, the Treasury of Gela at Olympia and

Temple C, Selinus, must have had them. They are also mentioned in several inscriptions. The Arsenal inscription gives their dimensions as 15 cm. wide, 3 cm. high, and 8 cm. apart. The Gallery inscription will permit either boards laid on top of the rafters, or more substantial members rabbeted into them. The dimensions are not given, but they are to be about 30 cm. apart (a much less closely knit structure than the Arsenal). The cuttings in the Pinakotheke are on an average about 25 cm. wide and 38 cm. apart, but they vary quite a lot.

It is possible that sometimes battens were laid in a continuous deck. Tiles could then either be laid on the battens direct or with a clay layer in between, as in Maiuri's reconstruction of the Casa del Telaio at Herculaneum. This is the only building where there is anything like actual evidence for such a structure, but Rodenwaldt (*Korkyra*, I, fig. 43) restores it for the Temple of Artemis on Corcyra (presumably wanting to restore sheathing and clay but not having enough room).

4. TILES, RAFTERS, PURLINS. Modern technique, as exemplified in Pl. IX*d*, shows that such a structure is possible practically, and the very limited space free for the timbers in many ancient buildings suggests that then, too, it was in use. We have already noted how in only one of the four buildings studied in detail is there enough space for battens, and we find ourselves faced with the same problem time and time again. It is very common to find that there is no room for a batten strong enough to matter unless it is rabbeted into the sides of the rafter instead of laid on top of it; and this weakens the rafter.

A typical example is the Sicyonian Treasury at Olympia (see Pl. XI*d*). Fig. 17*a* shows it as I believe it to have been. Below is Doerpfeld's restoration. It will be seen how the complex of battens and sheathing that he held to be necessary has the effect of forcing the rafter level down, until instead of landing on the flat top of the cornice block they have to be fitted round the corner of it. This results in a large V-shaped bite being cut out of the end of the rafter. I do not like it. I think that under the weight of the tiles above there would be a considerable risk of a crack starting at the apex of the V and running back up the rafter. Moreover, the rafters are so low that they are touching the ceiling beams. This leaves Doerpfeld no space to lay any boarding on top, so that the slots between the beams perforce remain open, giving a most peculiar ceiling. The upper half of the figure shows how these difficulties vanish if we lay the tiles directly on the rafters.

An even plainer exposition of the perils attendant on the insistence on battens in unsuitable circumstances may be seen in Fiechter's restoration of Aphaia.[1] Here only 13 cm. is available for the secondary timbers. Fiechter, however, insists on cramming in battens, sheathing, and clay. This brings the rafters down to a mere

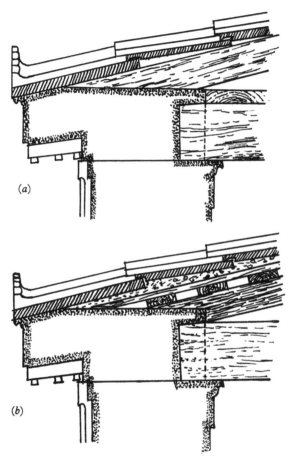

Fig. 17. Sicyonian Treasury, Olympia. (a) Present study; (b) after Doerpfeld.

6 cm. thick, and these had to carry the weight of battens, sheathing, clay and tiles over a span of 1·90 m. The impossibility of such a structure is manifest, and we may accept with confidence the restoration of Cockerell,[2] who uses rafters alone, as infinitely more likely to be right.

To these may be added the Treasury of Cyrene at Delphi, where the space free for the secondary timbers is 10 cm. (as measured from the rafter cuttings in the cornice blocks), and the Temple of Nemesis at Rhamnous (see Appendix II). The purlin sockets in the Temple at Kardaki (Fig. 13) show that there there was about 12·5 cm. free for the secondary timbers, but this is not conclusive, for Kardaki had a Gaggera roof, and this could be covered by relatively light rafters. Battens would therefore be possible, though they would have to be fairly light; nevertheless, Rodenwaldt[1] contrives to fit them in in the Temple of Artemis, where the space is about the same.

Another possible but not too reliable indication of the tiles having been sometimes laid on the rafters is to be found in the tiles themselves. The normal pantile is of the same thickness throughout its length. This means that its underside touches the rafter only at the top end of the tile, the bottom resting on the next tile below it in a watertight overlap. Occasionally, however, buildings have been published roofed with a wedge-shaped pantile the thickness of which increases towards the lower edge. The result of this is that the underside of the tile remains in contact with the rafter throughout its length; the whole row of tiles, in fact, presents an unbroken flat underside from ridge to eaves. Such technique hints strongly at the tiles lying directly on the rafters.

Nevertheless, this evidence seems a trifle unreliable, for I can never be quite sure that the wedge-shaped pantiles published in support of it[2] do not, in fact, come from the raking cornice. There tiles normally lay flat on the raking cornice blocks and could logically be wedge-shaped so as to lie on them easily, though being of the normal type through the rest of the building.[3]

Yet another argument against the use of battens is furnished by the cornice block from Delphi shown in Pl. IX*b* which, as we have noted, seems to indicate a continuous deck of rafters. Such a technique was most unusual, but at least it would in no circumstances require the addition of battens or sheathing. Possibly it was meant to be seen from inside as a sloped ceiling.

A final piece of evidence to support the rafters-only theory is the pierced tile. These are relatively common in Greek architecture. Dinsmoor[4] lists such tiles as having been found at Olympia, Athens, Kalydon, Olynthus, Corinth, Tegea, Bassae, Colophon, Priene, Sybaris, Caulonia, and Pompeii. To this formidable list I may add that illustrated (Pl. XIII*d*), which is in the little museum on the site at Epipoli, near Syracuse.

The sum total of this is that pierced tiles existed, and existed over a very wide field. Their purpose is usually given as lighting the attic and ventilating the timbers. Certainly ventilation seems to have been their main function, for we find them sometimes, especially at Pompeii, covered with little cupolas, so that very little light is admitted. This doubtless also explains their presence in such buildings as Bassae, where, in the absence of a stairway or any obvious site for one, we must assume that the attic was very little used and so would not really require lighting. In fact, I must admit that I am rather surprised that Bassae had any pierced tiles at all.[1] The temple is in the wettest part of Greece and is subject to rainstorms that can be of quite devastating ferocity. That holes should be left open in the roof, even allowing that the raised lip round the edge of the hole would divert water running down the slope and admit only the rain falling directly over the hole, seems odd. Possibly there was some sort of detachable lid that could be applied at the beginning of winter; it would have to be applied from inside, for once the builder's scaffolding was down there would be no way on to the top of the roof.

There is no reason why pierced tiles should not be used with sheathing and battens, but this would require the construction of a light well, as it were, through the secondary timbers under every pierced tile. On the other hand, no alterations would be needed if the structure was one of rafters and battens, or rafters alone.

Having passed these remarks on the pierced tile perhaps we may now digress and add a few words about its big brother, the opaion. The hypaethral heresy, as it has aptly been termed, no longer holds the ground that it did. It is valid for a few exceptions, namely the monster temples of the East, which it is quite certain were hypaethral, and the two colossi of Sicily, G Selinus and the Olympieion at Agrigento. These are both somewhat doubtful. The presence of an inside colonnade in G Selinus might indicate at least a hope that somehow the cella might be spanned, but the columns are very small, and the naiskos so reminiscent of that in the Didymaion at Miletos that I am inclined to believe it hypaethral. The Olympieion too seems never to have had a roof, though one may perhaps have been planned.[2]

Apart from these there were no hypaethral temples in Greece or Sicily. None of the remaining buildings have any sign of a drain to carry the water away from the cella floor, nor would one expect the many costly offerings to be exposed to the elements, least of all the chryselephantine statue at Olympia. No actual concrete evidence has ever been brought forward in favour of a hypaethral cella, except by Orlandos, who, in *A. Delt.* 1923, restores one at Stratos on the strength of a fragment of Ionic cornice. Pl. XIV c, however, shows the top of this cornice fragment to be quite rough, making impossible the restoration of Orlandos, who lays a sima on top of it, running around the inside of the opaion. Moreover, the cella has no escape drain to carry away the water, but instead a sill across the doorway that would keep it inside. The hypaethral cella is therefore to be rejected.

5. TILES, PURLINS. Most of the evidence for this structure has already been set out and need not be repeated. The most important feature is the slight tilting of the purlins at Aphaia, already noted on p. 52. We may here note in addition that this system was there applied to a roof of terra-cotta tiles, which seems to explode the theory that terra-cotta tiles always had to lie in a clay bed. At Gaggera too we have seen that the tiles probably lay directly on the purlins (pp. 18 ff.). Was this practice widespread? I do not think so. Two conditions must be fulfilled if a building is to be roofed in this way: the purlins must be sited high, close up under the tiles, and they must be set on the tile spacing. Bearing this in mind let us consider Table 3 (p. 53).

The Temples of Artemis and Kardaki on Corcyra are ruled out immediately by having closed purlin sockets, showing that the purlins did not come up to roof level. C Selinus can safely be forgotten; entirely apart from the testimony of K & P, fig. 77 on the irregular spacing of the purlins, there is the irregular spacing of the rafter sockets along the side cornice, pointing to a roof of battens and sheathing. Concord, Agrigento has already been dealt with (pp. 26 f.). Hera, Agrigento is very doubtful in every way. E Selinus is also doubtful. Next come the Metroon and the Temple of Zeus at Olympia. The first of these has the cuttings set rather wide apart— 90 cm. interaxial—and sited low. The second looks more hopeful, but the interaxial spacing (89 cm.) does not match the tile length as given by Doerpfeld (about 70 cm.). Crimisa also is doubtful, and its purlins seem to be sited low. We have thus disposed of every building on the list except Aphaia and the Megaron itself.

What conclusions are we to draw from this evidence? The chief one is that there seem to have been as many different techniques in the ancient world as in the modern. One fact, however, stands out. It is that the terra-cotta tile could be treated relatively roughly and did not really need the clay layer so often supposed inseparable from it. We have seen how both at Aphaia and at Gaggera it could be laid direct on the purlins without even the use of rafters.

I would suggest that clay may have been used with early buildings (Treasury of Gela, C Selinus), and possibly later with large Laconian tiles. In classical work it may have been used for little more than filling and packing around awkward joints. In many buildings, particularly the smaller, the tiles lay direct on the rafters. They could also lie directly on the purlins of a Gaggera roof, but this was less common. There seems to be no justification for the rule demanding more careful treatment for terra-cotta than for marble tiles. Battens were in use both with marble and terra-cotta tiles. Finally, we may point out, in a great number of buildings we still cannot say which of these systems was employed.

VIII

THE DEVELOPMENT OF CORNICE BLOCKS

Having considered the rafters and the various subsidiary members that could be built on top of them we may now examine the way in which the rafters were related to the walls and entablature of the temple; this involves us in a study of the various ways in which the side cornice blocks could be treated.

The earliest cornice members known are of very simple design. They are little more than a large, flat terra-cotta slab projecting from the top of the entablature with its soffit curved down into an overhanging lip designed to carry the rain out so as to drip down free of the walls. Typical early cornices of this sort, from Thermon and Kalydon,[1] are shown in Fig. 18.

All the surrounding members except the tiles were of wood, and, except for a few nail holes, there is no evidence for the relation of cornice to roof and entablature. In shape they resemble the normal Doric raking cornice, and the side cornice not at all. Presumably these slabs were set level; certainly, judging from their profiles, those from Thermon and B 2 Kalydon could well be either set on a slope or laid flat, but that from B 1 Kalydon could never be set on a slope.[2] It is hard to say on the evidence of these slabs alone whether the tiles on top of them were laid flat to form a Chinese roof or set on the slope, but there seems to be at least some evidence supporting the Chinese roof (pace Dinsmoor),[3] and certainly if the tiles were set on the slope one would expect, on the analogy of later buildings, the top outer edge of the cornice slab to be shaved off at an angle to provide a bed for the sloping underside of the sima.[4] The rafters probably sloped down to find a bed on the upper surface of the cornice slab, or, in the event of a Chinese roof, behind it.

The next step, demonstrated by Temple A Kalydon, is the transition into stone. The cornice block retains the form of a broad, thin slab, with the rafters presumably supported on its upper surface. The same scheme is to be observed in various archaic cornices from Selinus published by Gabrici.[5]

76

About this time, however, the shape of the cornice block underwent a radical alteration, and the flat-slab type, harking back to a terra-cotta original, was replaced by one of more orthodox proportions. The change was only to be expected, for the old terra-cotta form did not readily lend itself to reproduction in stone, and the more logically shaped blocks in the coursed masonry of the walls, which, of course, also came in with the transition to stone, provided a ready model for the new style. We see the change in several of the cornices from Selinus,[1] which now become the solid foursquare blocks to which we are accustomed.

The change brought with it a dilemma over the bedding of the rafters. They could still run down, as before, on to the upper surface of the cornice block, though the fact that the outer edge was now invariably cut on the slope to provide a bed for the sima slightly reduced the field available. Alternatively, it was possible to cut the whole top of the block on the slope of the roof; then the tiles could be laid on it direct and the rafters accommodated in a row of individual sockets cut for them along the top inside edge of the block. These two types of cornice block, in one form or another, are to be found throughout the history of Greek architecture. They can generally be distinguished from each other, and though natural development often evolves a form standing almost midway between the two, we can usually see from which side it evolved. I have divided my drawings on this plan, and Fig. 18 shows those blocks in which the entablature is conceived of as having a flat top with the rafters sloping down on to it from above, while Fig. 19 shows those where the entablature is carried up to roof level throughout its width, and the rafters run into sockets at the upper corner. Neither category can be assigned rigidly to any particular place or time, but we may note that, on the whole, the western Greeks tended to employ the sloping-topped type, while a rather special type of flat-topped block came into use in Periclean Athens.

Within the category of flat-topped blocks several variants can be distinguished. A common one is that represented by the second of the two Selinus cornices shown, the cornice from Delphi,[2] and that of Temple C Selinus. In these the rafters were accommodated in sloping cuttings in the top of the block, instead of lying flat on it. The Delphi cornice, as has already been noted, apparently had a continuous deck of rafters, so that the cuttings form a long, unbroken depression.[3]

The cuttings for the rafters in Temple C Selinus have also been commented on (p. 60). The cuttings are published both by Gabrici and K & P.[4] K & P, however,

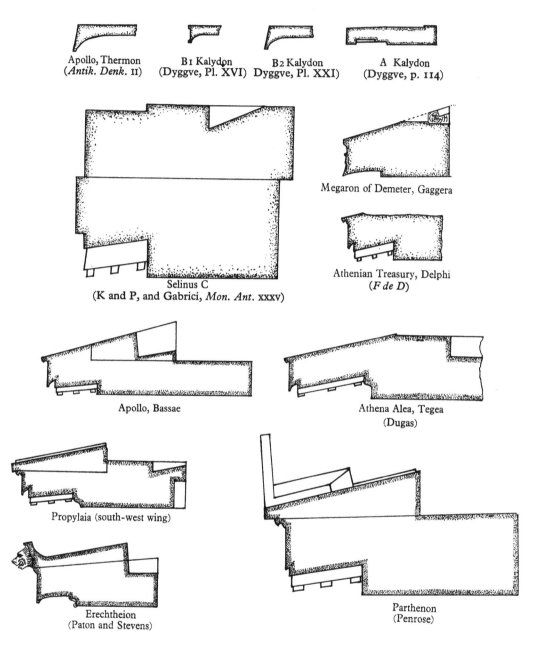

Apollo, Thermon
(*Antik. Denk.* II)

B1 Kalydon
(Dyggve, Pl. XVI)

B2 Kalydon
Dyggve, Pl. XXI)

A Kalydon
(Dyggve, p. 114)

Selinus C
(K and P, and Gabrici, *Mon. Ant.* xxxv)

Megaron of Demeter, Gaggera

Athenian Treasury, Delphi
(*F de D*)

Apollo, Bassae

Athena Alea, Tegea
(Dugas)

Propylaia (south-west wing)

Erechtheion
(Paton and Stevens)

Parthenon
(Penrose)

Fig. 18 (and opposite). Cornice blocks—I.

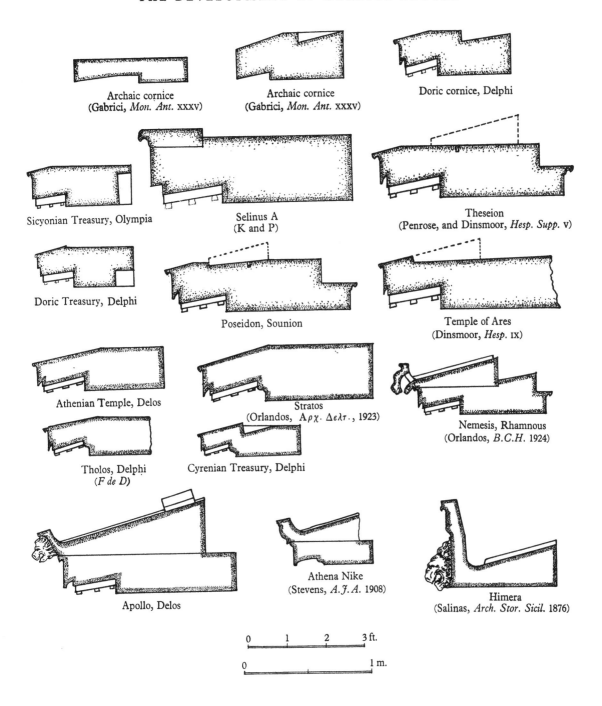

Archaic cornice
(Gabrici, *Mon. Ant.* xxxv)

Archaic cornice
(Gabrici, *Mon. Ant.* xxxv)

Doric cornice, Delphi

Sicyonian Treasury, Olympia

Selinus A
(K and P)

Theseion
(Penrose, and Dinsmoor, *Hesp. Supp.* v)

Doric Treasury, Delphi

Poseidon, Sounion

Temple of Ares
(Dinsmoor, *Hesp.* ix)

Athenian Temple, Delos

Stratos
(Orlandos, Αρχ. Δελτ., 1923)

Nemesis, Rhamnous
(Orlandos, *B.C.H.* 1924)

Tholos, Delphi
(*F de D*)

Cyrenian Treasury, Delphi

Apollo, Delos

Athena Nike
(Stevens, *A.J.A.* 1908)

Himera
(Salinas, *Arch. Stor. Sicil.* 1876)

0   1   2   3 ft.

0   1 m.

79

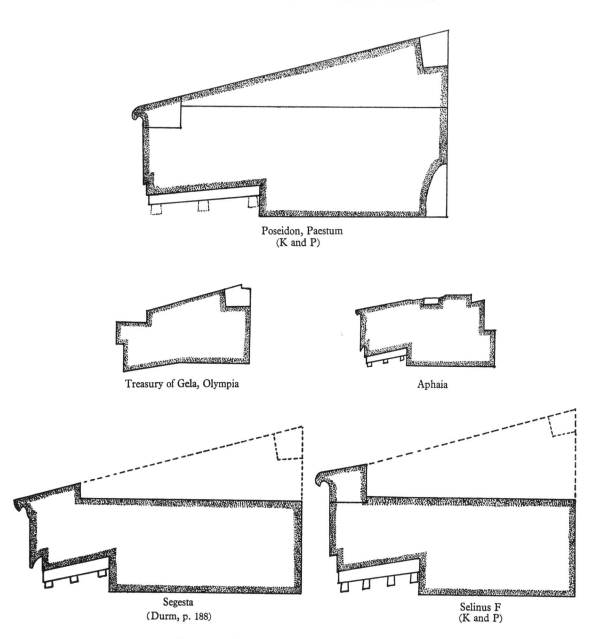

Poseidon, Paestum
(K and P)

Treasury of Gela, Olympia

Aphaia

Segesta
(Durm, p. 188)

Selinus F
(K and P)

Fig. 19 (and opposite). Cornice blocks—II.

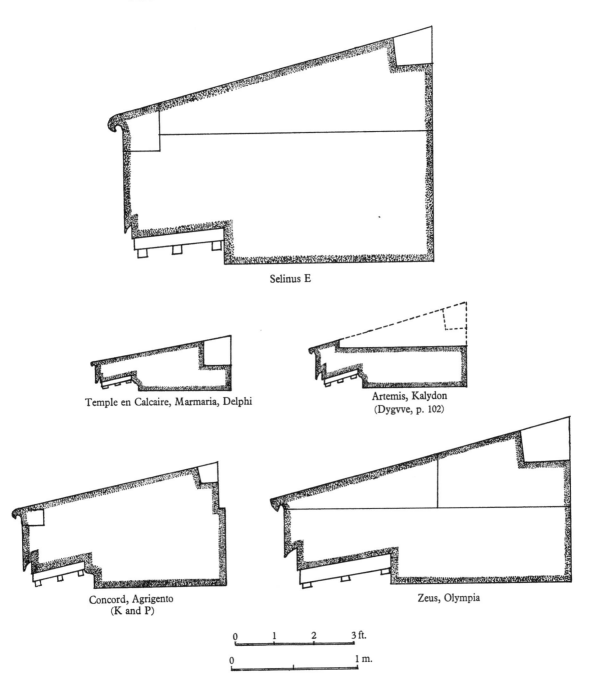

Selinus E

Temple en Calcaire, Marmaria, Delphi

Artemis, Kalydon
(Dygvve, p. 102)

Concord, Agrigento
(K and P)

Zeus, Olympia

0   1   2   3 ft.

0   1 m.

interpreted the rafter cuttings as notches cut to take the ends of the tiles (which would thus form a Chinese roof), and made no provision for the support of the rafters at all.

There was also another quite different school of thought in the treatment of cornice blocks, apparently holding that since it was easier to cut the wood to fit the stonework than vice versa the block should be left in its natural square shape and the rafters cut to fit on or around it. The Megaron of Demeter at Gaggera had a cornice of this type, for though the top was flattened off to take the rafters there were no sockets of any kind cut for them. As we have already seen,[1] the rafters were here probably treated in a rather special way, being rabbeted into the side of a wooden wall-plate rather than cut into a taper so as to rest direct on the stone. This was more usual and was apparently the system employed in another three buildings shown: the Athenian Treasury at Delphi, the Sicyonian Treasury at Olympia, and a Doric building at Delphi. The Athenian Treasury is indeed an excellent example of the policy of 'letting the wood take care of itself', for, with the exception of the narrow strip smoothed off to take the eaves tile, the rest of the block has been left very rough indeed, without the slightest attempt to adapt it to the woodwork. So rough a finish is most unusual and is not found in the other two blocks under consideration, both of which have their tops carefully smoothed. There is no indication on either where the rafters went, and they were presumably laid directly on top.[2]

Another block of this type is the cornice of the Temple of Kardaki (Fig. 13). This type of cornice with a flat top and no sockets cut for the rafters was one of the commonest of all designs, and its use extended over a very long period. According to K & P, whose interpretation I reproduce in Fig. 18, it was used in Temple A, Selinus. However, I found on the site a wedge-shaped block, similar to the upper member of the cornice of E Selinus; and so it is quite possible that, like it, Temple A also had a sloping-topped cornice. The block is of the correct measurements to combine satisfactorily with the elements shown by K & P.

Next we have to deal with the cornices of three buildings which, it is generally agreed, were designed by the same architect—the Theseion, the Temple of Poseidon at Sounion, and the Temple of Ares; the fourth building attributed to him, the Temple of Nemesis at Rhamnous, will be considered later. It has well been remarked by Plommer[3] that 'a good architect often reverts several times to the same formal and constructional problems'. This is well illustrated by these three cornice blocks, which, if we omit the various members restored on top of them (which are conjectural anyhow), show a very close family likeness indeed. At the same time they present a difficult problem, which may be termed the problem of the wedge-shaped course. This problem is represented by the cornice blocks of the Theseion and the temples of Poseidon at Sounion, Athena Alea at Tegea, and Zeus at Nemea. In each the cornice is flat-topped and carries at regular intervals dowels that fastened something to the flat top. The problem consists in deciding what that something was.

The evidence for the Theseion has already been reviewed (p. 15) and seems to point quite definitely to a course of masonry. At Sounion the evidence seems largely the same. The only difference is that this time the top of the cornice blocks is sloped slightly downwards, so as to provide a slight lip at the front for the wedge block to abut against, thereby giving it a more stable base. This time it was Orlandos who first called attention to the dowels,[1] and, rejecting the idea that they fastened the ends of the rafters themselves to the cornice blocks, restored instead the course of wedge-shaped blocks that Dinsmoor was later to suggest for the Theseion.[2]

Of the Temple of Ares only the shape of the cornice itself is known. There are three alternatives: the rafters may have run on to it direct, as in, for example, the Sicyonian Treasury at Olympia; there may have been a course of plain masonry, as in the Theseion; or there may have been a course of masonry carrying sockets for the rafters, as at Bassae. The analogy of both Sounion and the Theseion seems to point to the second, and I have dotted it in so on my drawing (Fig. 18). True, there is nothing in either the Temple of Ares or the Theseion to show whether the wedge block carried rafter sockets or not, but at Sounion, where its size is indicated by the extent of the sloping bed, it is plainly too small. For the sake of consistency I have restored the same system throughout.

The technique employed in the Temple of Apollo at Bassae was something similar, with the exception that here the wedge blocks are still to be found, and carry definite sockets for the rafters.[3] It shares the same general treatment as the preceding three examples, for points of resemblance greatly outnumber points of divergence, as may be seen by comparison with a building such as the Temple of Poseidon at Paestum. There may at first sight appear to be an affinity between Bassae and Paestum, but closer consideration will show that the two temples are in fact approaching a common form from opposite directions, for at Bassae the cornice is primarily a flat-topped one with a sloping section added, while at Paestum the whole thickness of the entablature is carried up to roof level.

6-2

Tegea and Nemea tell a different story. Their cornice blocks are almost the same in design. Of the two, only Tegea has been published;[1] Nemea is shown in Fig. 20 and Pl. IX a. It will be seen that the lower parts of the rafters are held in individual sockets, and that once again there is a row of dowels, one opposite each rafter. These Dugas uses to fix the ends of the rafters to the cornice, thus giving the rafter a V-shaped end. I must confess that I am tempted to give the rafters a normal square end and stop them in the sockets; then the dowels could be used to hold a course of small wedge blocks, especially as, judging from Dugas's extremely careful drawing of the blocks (I have not myself seen any of the actual stones), the top is dressed smooth with some care, in the manner of a block that is to have another course laid

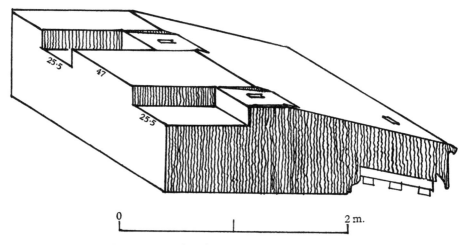

Fig. 20. Temple of Zeus, Nemea. Side cornice.

on top of it. At Tegea, however, there is hardly room for such a course; even assuming that it were laid with T-shaped blocks which as well as stopping the heads of the rafters also ran back and filled the spaces between them, they would be rather flimsy and futile. Dugas's solution seems the more probable, and is borne out by Nemea. There the dowels are set in the middle of slight, shallow channels that are cut opposite each rafter socket and in continuation of it. This certainly does suggest that the dowels were meant for the ends of the rafters, as Dugas suggests for Tegea; moreover, of these dowels Mr B. H. Hill, who has made a detailed study of Nemea, writes to me: 'I haven't seriously considered exactly what shape the objects dowelled at the lower end of the rafters had. Their purpose was most probably to hold the rafters *down* firmly. It would be easy to contrive a contraption that would serve, and that could be leaded before the rafter was put in place.'

A course of continuous stonework is quite excluded. The only other explanation of the dowels at all possible is a series of little stone blocks stopping the rafters, such as have been restored in the Temple of Aphaia (p. 87). I must, however, confess that Dugas's solution is much more probable, both for Tegea and for Nemea.

If he is correct, then these are the only two places I know where wood was dowelled with the long-shaped dowels normally reserved for use with masonry. I should have thought that there might be a risk that these long dowels would start a crack in the beam, especially as they would be set in one of the thinnest parts of it; and in any case, if dowels were to be used with the rafters, why not set them in the bottoms of the rafter sockets? This would be a much more natural place for them. All in all, I am not happy about these two buildings. Certainly their evidence is not such as to induce me to dowel the rafters to the cornice at Sounion, where I follow Orlandos in restoring wedge blocks with a confidence that is marred only by the disturbing fact that neither at Sounion nor in the Theseion, otherwise so well preserved, has a single fragment of a wedge block been found.

After the uncertainties of Tegea and Nemea it is encouraging to find blocks once more falling into the category that we have called flat-topped. Such are the cornices of the Temple of the Athenians at Delos, the Tholos at Delphi, the Temple at Stratos, and, finally, the Treasury of Cyrene at Delphi. These are all treated in the same way, with the exceptions that in the Temple of the Athenians the rafters were probably unusually slight,[1] and in the Treasury of Cyrene ran into sloping sockets, as in C Selinus, instead of tapering off into a point.

It is now time to return to the Athens of Pericles to trace the development of a specialized form of flat-topped block that came into vogue around then. We have seen how in the hands of the Theseion architect the cornice block came to carry a low wedge-shaped course that both stopped the rafters and supported the tiles. The next step originated in the fertile brain of either Mnesicles or Ictinos, for in both the Parthenon and the Propylaia the separate tile is discarded, and instead the wedge block itself has its upper surface cut into a representation of a pair of pantiles, so that block and tile become one. This unit is generally referred to as an eaves tile, but here again we suffer from the lack of a standard terminology and the term is sometimes applied (strictly speaking more correctly) to orthodox tiles as well. This new system became standard in Periclean Athens, and was adopted, with only slight differences, for the Parthenon, the Propylaia, the Erechtheion, the Temple of Nemesis at Rhamnous, and the little Temple of Athena Nike. It remained in vogue for a very long time, and we meet it in the Temple of Apollo on Delos and also in the Propylaia at Eleusis (not illustrated).

The treatment of the rafters varied. They could either be supported directly on the cornice, after the style of the flat-topped blocks, with their heads resting against the eaves blocks, or, to make assurance double sure, they could have their lower half accommodated in a sloping socket cut in the cornice block. The Propylaia, indeed, used both systems.[1] It was a natural development out of what had gone before, and when we compare the cornices of the Theseion and the Temple at Rhamnous it is not hard to see how one could grow out of the other. This must not be taken as meaning that the eaves block was invented by the Theseion architect; most writers agree on making the Rhamnous temple later than the Parthenon and the Propylaia, in which it is already in existence. If this is right, then the credit must go to Ictinos or Mnesicles, and Rhamnous is the copy, not the prototype. It did not, however, involve the Theseion architect in any great change from the design to which he was accustomed.

So far development has been reasonably logical. We have seen how the flat-topped block came to carry a low supplementary course of masonry to stop the rafters and support the tiles; we have seen how in Athens the next step was taken and the wedge blocks and tiles fused into one. It is at this point that logical progression ceases and we are faced with the Temple of Victory at Himera. Here we find an eaves block on the Athenian model distant both in space and time.[2] By the laws of reason it has no right to exist at all, but it is a mistake to guide one's footsteps too inflexibly by the rule of logic, for most rules have their exceptions, and that is what we have come across here. It is not the only exception, for the Olympieion at Agrigento also seems to have had the tops of its cornice blocks cut roughly into the shape of tiles. Probably therefore we are to see in this an anticipation of Athenian practice in early fifth-century Sicily. One would expect the sloping-topped cornices in use in the West to lend themselves to such a technique more readily than the flat-topped blocks of Greece, but in fact it never seems to have spread beyond a small isolated pocket, and we find that all the large western temples continued to have the tiles laid on the cornice as a separate unit.

The buildings where the cornice had a sloping top are rather fewer in number and are more uniform in treatment. They are shown in Fig. 19. The earliest is the Treasury of Gela at Olympia. We have already discussed this building and the manifold problems that it presents.[1] The general scheme is clear enough. The top of the block sloped up at the same roof angle as is given by the tympanum slabs.[2] The rafters were stopped in a series of sockets cut in the top corner of the block, as usual.

The next building in chronological sequence is the Temple of Aphaia. This too has certain peculiarities. There are two steps cut into the inside face of its cornice blocks. The lower, which is horizontal, carried the ceiling (the moulding being on a separate course laid alongside), while the upper, being sloped, must have carried the ends of the rafters. This is a continuous cutting and not a series of individual sockets. The top of the block is well enough smoothed off at its outer and inner edges; in the centre is a strip left rather rough, and in the centre of this strip a row of holes or sinkings. They had evidently nothing to do with the lifting of the block into place—it is provided with channels for lifting loops. The two publications of the temple agree[3] in making them the sockets for stone blocks or pegs. Cockerell ran the bottom of his rafters on to the inclined step or ledge, and the top on across the cornice block to abut against the stone peg. Fiechter, on the other hand, as a result of restoring battens and clay, found that his rafters were so thin that the top would not clear the edge of the cornice block, and so could not be made to reach the peg. Accordingly he could find no other purpose for them than to prop up the first row of tiles so that they stand clear of the cornice block.

Neither of these restorations seems particularly likely, chiefly because of the stone pegs, which are a most unorthodox piece of construction whatever the explanation. It bears all the signs of being some kind of makeshift; perhaps an error was made in the cutting of the cornice blocks, and it was not until they were all in place that it was discovered that their tops had been cut too low, so that if the tiles were laid on them as had been planned they would be lying at too shallow an angle, making it impossible to link them to those on the raking cornice at each end, which would be at the correct slope. Accordingly the pegs were inserted as a last-minute expedient to bring up the level of the cornice blocks where necessary. They may also have had the rafters stopped against them, as Cockerell suggests. But the truth is that I am not really satisfied with anybody's explanation of these pegs, including my own.

If the first two buildings in our catalogue of sloping-topped cornices are rather unorthodox, there is a truly remarkable degree of uniformity in the rest. Temples F and E at Selinus, Poseidon at Paestum, Zeus at Olympia, Concord at Agrigento, and the 'Temple en Calcaire' at Delphi—all these show surprisingly little difference in the structure of their cornices. They are all so much alike that there is little to be said, but we must call attention to the presence in the list of Zeus at Olympia. This is the only known example of this type of cornice block among the large buildings of Greece proper. True, it does appear later in the 'Temple en Calcaire', and in both the Propylaia and the Katagogion at Epidauros, but these are hardly good parallels to the Temple of Zeus. I do not suppose that this has any particular significance. Every rule has its exceptions, and the general tendency of development is fairly clearly established by the other buildings. There is no reason why the architect should not have done things differently, once in a while.

The two buildings remaining, the Temple of Artemis at Kalydon and the Temple at Segesta, are somewhat conjectural as far as the cornice is concerned. At Kalydon only a small piece of the wedge block is preserved, from the thin end, and therefore giving no indication whether the block was provided with rafter sockets or left plain, as restored in the Theseion. I have restored it with sockets, but this could well be wrong. If it is right it would provide a parallel to the Temple of Zeus at Olympia.

The Temple of Segesta has never been properly published or studied. The only sections of the cornice available to me were the very small-scale one published by Durm,[1] and that faintly dotted in on the drawing of the entablature printed by K & P, and described as being 'nach Hittorf'. In any case the general situation is plain: the cornice has a flat top, and if there were ever any wedge blocks on top of it there are none there now. Neither of the publications shows whether there are any signs of dowels that could point to an additional course. The upturned lip of the cornice seems to show that a second course was planned, for when a course of wedge blocks was to be laid the cornice was generally treated in this way. At the same time a flat top is not impossible, though it would be the only one among all large West Greek buildings.

This is a reasonably complete summary of the types of cornice structure to be found in western and mainland Greek temples in the archaic and classical periods. There have none the less been several omissions. Some, like the Propylaia at Gaggera, are left out because they simply duplicate systems already well attested (the Propylaia had a flat-top cornice like that of the Athenian Temple on Delos); others do not appear because the evidence seemed insufficient or was not available. In particular I have been unable to include the Temple of Ceres at Paestum because all the relevant blocks were lying on the ground upside down, so that I was unable to measure or examine them closely. They seem to have some kind of sloping top, but how far back the slope extends I should not care to say. I have also passed over the two giant temples in Sicily, G Selinus and the Olympieion at Agrigento, because the evidence for the cornice of each of them is very fragmentary.

Although not strictly concerned with woodwork, while we are dealing with cornice blocks we can scarcely avoid some mention of the Chinese roof. This has been the subject of prolonged controversy. The various buildings alleged to have had it are listed by Dinsmoor,[1] only to be firmly rejected. He names five sites in all: Kalydon, Ephesos, C Selinus, Eretria, and Ceres at Paestum. Of these, he is certainly right to reject Paestum, for I examined the angle cornice blocks and Krauss[2] has described and interpreted them correctly. Of the remaining four, Selinus is dismissed as 'illogical', leaving three. These three are summarily disposed of with the enigmatic remark 'the two (sic) other substances are conjectural'.

Of Ephesos I have nothing to say. Eretria is based on an acroterion base quoted by Studniczka in AA, 1912, 323, which has a level bottom, and therefore, if the statue it supported was not to lean outwards, must have rested on a level section of the roof. I was unable to find this piece in a search of the museums of Eretria and Chalcis, both of which are in some disorder.

Kalydon is attested by a similar angle block carrying a base for an acroterion, in this case a sphinx.[3] On the surface this looks very convincing, and I could wish that Dinsmoor had been more explicit in his rejection of it.

C Selinus I think is more doubtful. As we have seen, the irregularity of the rafter spacing presupposes a layer of sheathing, and probably clay too. From Gabrici[4] it is clear that, given the rafter level set by the existing cuttings, the secondary timbers must be fairly thin if the first row of tiles is to lie flat to form a Chinese roof. He restores only rafters and battens (which is a very doubtful construction for a building with such irregular timbers) and even so his woodwork is too thick to let the tiles lie flat. It seems, therefore, that if, as was likely, the secondary timbers were fairly thick, the temple cannot have had a Chinese roof.

There is, however, other evidence unmentioned by Dinsmoor. First may be quoted the Basilica at Paestum. An angle section of terra-cotta sima attributed to it is now in the museum at Paestum. It shows exactly the same characteristics as the piece from Kalydon published by Dyggve: once more if the acroterion is to stand upright then the fragment must be so laid that the raking sima is horizontal. It is, of course, possible that the Basilica was a hip-roofed building, which would explain it away satisfactorily. This has been suggested by Choisy, p. 281.

But there is other evidence too. A small fragment of a temple model[1] now in the offices of the Soprintendenza alle Antichità at Salerno suggests that the edifice of which it formed part might have had a Chinese roof. Unfortunately, we cannot be sure that the flattened effect is not accidental, and the fragment terminates in a broken end just where it is beginning to get interesting.

No such fault mars another major find by Sestieri. This is the underground shrine uncovered at Paestum; it has not yet been properly published. The shrine is built completely of stone, and is in the form of a room two metres deep. The roof is formed by tiles laid on top of stone slabs acting as rafters. The whole was eventually covered over. This hardly gives us a roof of the normal type, but we can see that the stonework, by accident or design, gives a very fair representation of a Chinese roof (Pl. XII*a*, *b*). It would be wrong to conclude from this evidence that Chinese roofs actually existed, but at least it is strong enough to establish a definite possibility.

To summarize our results, there is no hard and fast rule for the distribution of one particular type of block in one particular time and place, but there does emerge a broad, general pattern. It starts in the flat terra-cotta cornice slabs of the earliest buildings, and after the translation into stone the block retains this flat top. The rafters sloping down to it may or may not be housed in sloping sockets. At Athens around the middle of the fifth century an additional wedge-shaped course appears on top, and soon this replaces the first row of tiles, having its own upper surface cut into their likeness; this technique has previously appeared at Agrigento, spreading to Himera, but was there never more than a short-lived local variant. It continued in use for a very long time, predominantly in Athenian work, while the orthodox flat-topped type continued in use parallel to it. In the western colonies there was meanwhile in use the sloping-topped block. It is perhaps conceivable that the origin of this difference is to be found in the early terra-cotta-revetted Sicilian temples, which had no flat cornice slab like their counterparts at Thermon and Kalydon, but had a rather more unified system of woodwork of which the sloping rafters formed an integral part. Be that as it may, there can be no denying that the sloping-topped block held sway predominantly in the West, and flat-topped in Greece proper. Exceptions to both rules occur. I have noted the more important, and no doubt more could be found; but as a general principle I believe that the rule set out above is supported by too great a volume of evidence to be seriously shaken; and though not nearly precise enough to serve in itself as a basis for dating a building I believe that cornice structure can be a useful confirmation in conjunction with other characteristics.

IX

TECHNIQUE

Before proceeding to some consideration of the various means by which the timbers might be joined both to each other and to the stone parts of the building, it will be well first to consider the timbers themselves. It would be wrong to say that in any given circumstances the Greeks would use timbers of any given shape or size, for their habits often varied, sometimes unaccountably. It may nevertheless be declared as a general principle that they liked beams bearing a heavy load to be as nearly square as possible. This is amply demonstrated by all the various cuttings for purlins and ridge beams that have been found, and the dimensions of which are set out in Table 2 (p. 46). The square cross-section was not rigidly adhered to, and we find beams either rather taller than they were wide (for example, Athenian Treasury at Delphi; Ceres, Paestum), or wider than they were tall (Sounion; Concord, Agrigento). The square beam nevertheless remains as the ideal behind all these variants. I imagine that the reasoning behind such a policy was no more than a feeling that the less was cut away from the original round log, the more was left to hold up the roof.

Of especial interest is the cornice block from the Temple of Aphaia already illustrated (Pl. VII c, Fig. 12 a). Although this is an open cutting it seems that the beam came right up to the top of it. This gives us a remarkably shaped beam, being 16 cm. wide by 28 cm. high. From this we might be tempted to wonder whether the Greeks could have grasped so early the vital fact that the strength of a beam lies in its depth, but this is unlikely. True, there are several other examples of beams being taller than they are wide, but in these the preponderance is not so marked, and we shall be reasonably safe if we put Aphaia down to chance. After all, if a man does not know which way up a beam should be laid, and there are only two alternatives possible, there is an even chance of him doing the right thing by accident.

That it was an accident seems to be proved by later history, for there is no continuation of such a technique, and it is not until Roman times that we find appearing regularly cuttings such as those shown in Pl. XIII c, the forum at Pompeii; until then it is the square beam that rules, and even in the Parthenon, where every ounce of strength was needed, we find no attempt to depart from it.

When we leave the heavy beams and consider the lighter members, things change slightly. Again, nothing can be asserted definitely. Rafters too were often nearly square, as we know from the Temple of Poseidon at Paestum. They were, however, just as often of a flattish cross-section, rather broader than they were high. Early reconstructions often show them thus relying on the equation of mutules and rafter ends. Supporting evidence is to be found in the representation of the rafters in the rock-cut tombs of the Etruscan necropolis of Cerveteri. The tombs often have their roofs cut into an appropriate representation of the roofing woodwork, and the rafters are invariably very broad and shallow indeed. The shallowness, and perhaps the breadth, is no doubt the result of a desire to make the stonecutting easier, which has the effect of flattening out the woodwork; but I would hesitate to accept this as the sole explanation of rafters 70 cm. broad and with gaps of about 15 cm. left between them.[1] Even allowing for the licence of the artist and the convenience of the mason, we must still believe that the original of the representation must have had rafters at least broader than the gaps between them. This implies that they were shallow in proportion, otherwise they would be impossibly heavy.

The same conclusions may be drawn from the stonework of certain Greek buildings. The rafter cuttings in the archaic cornice from Selinus (Fig. 18) are 22–33 cm. wide and about 17 cm. apart. The Treasury of Cyrene at Delphi had rafters 10 cm. thick and at least 15 cm. wide, as shown by the cuttings in the cornice blocks, while one of the most striking examples of all is furnished by no less a building than the Propylaia at Athens. Generally this building was constructed with flat-topped cornice blocks and wedge-shaped eaves blocks, the rafters resting on the first and abutting on the second, leaving no trace of their dimensions. But over the south-west wing the rafters were a little lower, or for some reason it was desired to give them an especially secure footing, and they were given individual sockets. These are shown in Pl. XIV b; the cuttings below them are for the beams of the slot ceiling. From these it appears that the rafters were quite exceptionally wide—nearly as wide as the tiles, in fact—and laid very close together. The sockets preserved are anything up to 50 cm. wide (possibly even larger),[2] and 16·3 cm. apart. Likewise, in the Temple of Concord (if we are to believe K & P, fig. 152) the rafters were much broader than they were deep (about 33 × 15 cm.). The Arsenal specification also tells us that there the rafters were about 37 cm. wide by 19 cm. high.

There were probably three reasons for this use of the flat rafter. One was strength. The rafter had to be made bigger, and, on a flat-topped cornice block, if the bottom of the rafter was too low it could not rest on the block (see Fig. 17). Second, a flat board lent itself very naturally to having other flattish members, such as battens and sheathing, nailed on top of it. The third and, I think, most important reason was the simple one of 'Why not?' A large beam could easily be sawn down the middle to give two rafters, each in the form of a plank; and, given a plank, what more natural than to lay it down flat?

As for the sockets into which the beams fitted, these were usually of parallel bore throughout. Dovetail sockets were however known, and there are three indisputable examples. These are the ridge beam of the Theseion (Fig. 5), the larger purlins of the Megaron of Demeter (Pl. V c), and the rafter sockets along the side cornice at Bassae. All of these are very noticeably wider at the back than at the mouth. There is one other socket in which the dovetailed effect is less pronounced, the ridge beam of the north Porch of the Erechtheion.[1] In the normal way a socket is dovetailed because the beam contained in it is going to be submitted to tension. This does not seem to have been the Greek idea, for it would hardly account for the dovetailing of the rafter sockets at Bassae, which is the last place in the whole building to be under tension, for the weight of the roof is pushing them down. We may therefore surely assume that the Greek architect used dovetails (which he did only rarely) not with the especial aim of resisting tension, but simply as a form of socket rather more secure than usual.[2] It is also not unknown to find a socket slightly wider at the top than the bottom to facilitate dropping the beam into place.[3]

The faces of the socket for a large beam are often left roughly striated or pock-marked, so as to give the wood something to get a grip on, but this is by no means always the case, and it is seldom done in the sockets for the lighter timbers. The distance that the socket was recessed into the stonework to provide a seating for the beam varies. Usually it is rather less than the width of the beam, varying between half and three-quarters of it, but there are a great many exceptions to this rule (see Table 2, p. 46). On occasion the seating could become quite drastically reduced, until it was a mere shelf. This happened at Paestum (p. 47) and in the

Theseion (pp. 10 f.). It would nevertheless be safe enough if the other end of the beam was firmly secured, to prevent it sliding out of the socket.

I know of no absolutely certain example in our period of wooden beams having been fixed to the stonework with dowels. No doubt it would be done with wall-plates, but I have yet to see a dowel that with complete and utter certainty was used to hold a beam.[1] The nearest thing to it is the dowels apparently holding the rafters to the cornice at Nemea (Pl. IX a). These admittedly are fairly sure, but I cannot rely on them completely. On the other hand, two of the purlin sockets of the Parthenon interrupt a clamp cutting in such a way that it seems certain that the other half of the clamp must have been embedded in the wooden beam, bonding it to the stone. I do not think they are old clamp cuttings in blocks re-used from the earlier Parthenon. The explanation is simply that the socket was cut after the blocks were in place; the clamp was originally intended to bond two blocks together, but then one of them was cut away to form the socket, half of the clamp cutting going with it and leaving the other half apparently clamping the stonework to the void.

It was probably usual to cut the beam sockets after the stonework was all in place. One indication of this is the interruption of clamp cuttings mentioned above. Another is furnished by the Temple of Segesta. Here, of the temple only the colonnade remains; indeed, it has been doubted whether the cella was ever built at all.[2] The colonnade, however, stands completed, except for the fluting and the removal of bosses and protective surfaces; it is nevertheless quite innocent of beam cuttings (Pl. XIV a), which it was evidently intended to add later.[3]

Three blocks from Temple E Selinus, one of which is shown in Pl. XV b,[4] however, argue in the opposite direction. It is a wedge block from the side cornice. Quite a number of these blocks are preserved, all carrying rafter sockets, which are 16·3 cm. wide and on an interaxial spacing of 65 cm. This means that each block usually carries two sockets. These particular three blocks, however, carry three and part of a fourth. They are of the correct size but are on an interaxial spacing of only 33 cm. Now it is hardly likely that over some part of the temple there should be twice as many rafters as usual, and the only other explanation possible is that two of the cuttings were made in error. It is even possible to guess how the error occurred. The two sockets which are wrong—which they are we cannot say—are on the correct spacing relative to each other, and are exactly half a tile width out. I would suggest that what happened was that someone went around the cornice blocks as they lay on the ground marking where the rafter sockets were to come. Somewhere, somehow, he got off sequence so that some of the sockets were cut on the wrong spacing before the mistake was noticed. The fact that the error was of exactly half of the normal interval suggests that possibly he was led astray by the block of non-standard length which, in most Doric temples, occurs at the mid-point of the side cornice, where the jointing of the blocks relative to the mutules below them changes over from one system to the other. The error was probably not noticed until the blocks were all up and in position, when the two extra cuttings were made to correct the discrepancy.[1]

This technique of cutting some of the sockets on the ground could only be adopted in later buildings. In early buildings, as we have seen, the disposition of the beam sockets, especially those for the rafters, is most irregular. This makes it plain that the woodwork was already being erected as the sockets were being cut, for they were plainly cut to fit the individual timbers that they were to house; nobody would dream of making a series of cuttings such as those in the cornice blocks of the Treasury of Gela and then scouring the country for beams to fit them. It is quite certain that the sockets were cut as the woodwork was actually built up. However, as the wood-work became more regular and uniform, the mason could safely anticipate the carpenter, at least to the extent of cutting sockets for beams not yet in place. The regularity of the rafter sockets in the Temple of Poseidon at Paestum, for example, would make it safe enough to cut them while the timbers were all still on the ground.

Of the tools used we know very little. It is often asserted that the ancients found it difficult to produce planks or flat boards, but this is wrong. First, there was ample experience of making boards to be gained in the trade of the shipwright. Second, there are numerous references to saws in inscriptions. Two types of saw seem to have been in use. There was the long cross-saw, the type used for felling trees and other jobs requiring no great fineness of execution. This was handled by two men, and was about 1·10 m. long by 15 cm. broad. It came into use in the eastern Mediterranean very early, for there are three of them in the museum at Heraklion, found in a Middle Minoan context. A peculiar feature is that none of the three has holes bored for handles at both ends; they appear at one end only. In two of the saws this might be through the holes having been in part of the metal that has corroded away, but of the third both ends seem to be intact. It must nevertheless have had a handle at each end, for it is too long and too easily bent to be used as a one-handed saw.

The second type of saw is one in frequent use by Greek joiners today. It is known as the bowsaw. The principle is that of the hacksaw; the blade is very thin and is held under tension in a wooden framework. This saw is used for smaller jobs, and can easily be used by one man, who holds one end of the framework in each hand as he saws. The use of this type in ancient times is attested by a representation of it in a wall-painting from Herculaneum now in the National Museum at Naples (no. 8991), showing carpenters at work. The artist has drawn the blade fixed in the middle of the framework instead of down one side, as in the normal modern saw, but the principle remains the same.

The same picture also shows a man at work with what would appear, from his attitude in using it, to be a plane. Adzes were also in common use, and many have been found; the head broadens out from the thin striking edge until at the hole for the handle it is almost square in cross-section; thus the adze can be turned on its side and used as a hammer.

As for the timbers themselves, the largest cuttings known are those for the Parthenon purlins, which were 93 cm. wide, and about 95 cm. high at the higher side. No doubt other timbers of equal size were used in the largest buildings, but a socket of such dimensions has to be cut out of not one block but several; once the pediment falls the socket is broken up and becomes unrecognizable. This is why the primary sockets in really large buildings are to be found only in those that are well preserved, while in smaller buildings the sockets, being often cut out of a single stone, survive even after the total collapse of the temple.

It is uncertain whether composite timbers were used. The only example that I know of is the conjectural one of the ridge beam of the Theseion, but temple accounts mention 'one-piece' and 'two-piece' timbers,[1] and I suppose this might refer to composite timbers.

We know little about how the timbers were joined to each other. Glue was often used. We also know from the Gallery inscription that the practice of rabbeting was known, for there it is suggested as a possible alternative to laying the battens flat on the rafters in the usual way. We know that it was also employed in more important joins, such as that between the rafters and the purlins. This is known from the high siting of certain of the purlins, which, if anything is to be deducted from their height to leave space for the rafters to lie on top of them, would have to be too shallow in proportion to their known width. Such beams are the outer purlins of the Temple

97

of Poseidon at Paestum, the ridge beam over the cella of the Temple of Ceres at Paestum, the purlins and ridge beam of the Parthenon, and, possibly, though I have not restored it so, the ridge beam of the Temple of Concord at Agrigento. In all of these the rafters must have been notched into the sides of the beams. The Arsenal inscription tells us that there the ridge beam was fastened to the crossbeams by a long pin passing right through a block that was laid in between.[1] References in inscriptions to both wooden pegs and iron nails are common. Moreover, the Phrygians at least had attained some skill in mortising timbers in architectural work.[2]

It is difficult to find by what Greek words the ancients referred to the various structures and techniques mentioned above; certainly the meaning of the Greek terms, as we meet them in the inscriptions, can seldom be determined with sufficient accuracy to justify our adoption of them in replacement of the conventional English names. Nevertheless, I have set out such evidence as is available in Appendix III.

PART III
APPENDICES

I

SLOT CEILINGS

As we have seen (pp. 36 ff.), the ceiling was often an integral and vital part of the roof construction. It will therefore be germane to our purpose to consider the various types of ceiling possible, and in particular one which, though in common use, has not as yet received the attention that is its due.

Of the normal stone ceiling our knowledge is reasonably complete, and we have fairly detailed epigraphical evidence for ceilings of wood.[1] The inscriptions all deal with a wooden ceiling of a design already known from its stone counterpart, that is, the coffer ceiling. On the strength of this evidence, when a wooden ceiling has to be restored it has become customary to restore a coffered one. There have been, it is true, exceptions to this,[2] but I have yet to see anyone call attention to the fact that there is widespread evidence that quite a different form of ceiling was in common use.[3]

The characteristic feature of this form of ceiling is that the cuttings or dressings for the ceiling beams show that they were too close together for coffers to be laid between them. Normally, indeed, there is no more than a narrow slot left open between the beams, which was presumably covered by light boarding laid on top of them. The slot is always much narrower than the ceiling beam, and the beams are much shallower in proportion to their width than the beams used with coffers. As I found this type of ceiling occurring in many different buildings I was forced to coin a name for it in order to facilitate reference; accordingly I shall speak of it as a 'slot ceiling', a term recalling one of its most prominent features.

There is evidence in the stonework that ceilings of this sort existed in the Sicyonian Treasury at Olympia, the Temple of Aphaia, the Temple of Ceres at Paestum, an unidentified Doric building at Delphi, the Temple at Kardaki on Corcyra, the Propylaia at Athens, and the Temple of Poseidon at Sounion. I also now believe that it was probably used in the Athenian Treasury at Delphi, and *RD*, p. 206, paras. 2 and 3, should be amended to that effect. Let us now consider the evidence for each of these buildings in turn. The measurements are set out in Table 4 below, and the blocks are drawn in Fig. 21.

SICYONIAN TREASURY AT OLYMPIA. Two cornice blocks are preserved in excellent condition: one is illustrated in Fig. 21 *a*. The ceiling cuttings were not carried on into the course below, the top of which carries the epikranitis moulding. In neither block are the beam sockets preserved for their full width, and there is no ready means of ascertaining how wide they were. We may, however, guess that they were not much wider than the left-hand socket in the block illustrated, which is 47·4 cm. wide. Doerpfeld gives no width in his restoration of the woodwork.[1] It is peculiar that the cuttings for these beams are slightly angled.[2] I cannot understand the reason for this. There is nothing to show whether this ceiling was used over the pronaos or the cella, but it is likely that the pronaos ceiling beams would run parallel to the axis of the building so as to take advantage of the shorter span; this would assign our blocks to the cella.

TABLE 4. SLOT CEILINGS

Measurements in centimetres

Building	Width of beam	Depth of beam	Width of slot
Sicyonian Treasury	47·4	25·5	11·5
Pinakotheke	46·5–52	25·5	14
South-west wing	47–53·5	28·5	14
Aphaia	47·3?	28	11·5–13·7
Kardaki	31–33	14·8?	24
Ceres, Paestum	66–76	30	33–46
Sounion	37	18	24·5
Doric, Delphi	19·5	13·3	12·5

THE PROPYLAIA. (A) SOUTH-WEST WING. The slot ceiling here is quite different and completely incontrovertible. A row of holes may be seen *in situ* on the south wall of the building,[3] providing sockets for ten ceiling beams. These beams are usually about 50 cm. wide, and vary in width by about 5 cm., with the exception of the last one to the east, which, with a width of only 23·5 cm., is half the width of the others.[4] The most interesting fact is that the whole course of masonry in the east wall corresponding to the level of the ceiling is slightly depressed and dressed in a manner suggesting that the ceiling was some-how in contact with it. The arangement of the beams seems to preclude this, for they lay parallel to this wall, and the last one (that is, the thin one) lay with its edge some distance out from the wall. The only thing that can possibly have abutted on the wall is the light boarding on top of the ceiling beams, and I cannot believe that a whole course was cut back to accommodate that. See Pl. XIII*b* and Fig. 21*c*.

The course joins on the north wall, which carried the other ends of the beams, do not coincide with those of the south wall, and only the lower halves of the beam sockets are preserved, the upper being contained in the cornice blocks, which are no longer *in situ*. These, however, correspond closely to those in the south wall, both in size and spacing.[5] Nine are preserved.

PROPYLAIA. (B) PINAKOTHEKE. The ceiling over the pronaos was similar to that over the south-west wing.[6] Cuttings are preserved on the crosswall between pronaos and cella

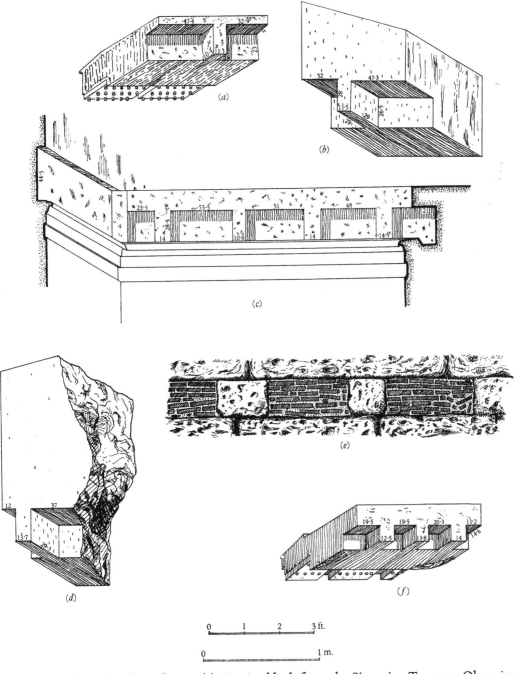

Fig. 21. Evidence for slot ceilings. (a) Cornice block from the Sicyonian Treasury, Olympia; (b) and (d) tympanum blocks from the Temple of Aphaia; (c) south-west wing of the Propylaia, showing sockets for ceiling beams; (e) bricked-up sockets in the west pediment of the Temple of Ceres, Paestum; (f) cornice block from a Doric building at Delphi.

on the same spacings that we have seen in the south-west wing. As in the north wall of the south-west wing, only the lower halves are preserved, to a depth of 9·5 cm. Some of the blocks of the course above can still be seen, though not *in situ*, and these carry the upper halves of the sockets, which are 16 cm. high, giving a total height of 25·5 cm. for the beams. They are 48 cm. wide, with slots about 14 cm. wide.

APHAIA. Several heavy tympanum blocks are to be found on the ground at the west end of the temple.[1] Two of them are shown in Fig. 21 *b* and *d*. The ceiling beam sockets are again plain to see, but, on these blocks, incomplete. They nevertheless give us a reasonably good idea of what the beams looked like.[2] Their proportions are much the same as those of the Propylaia and the Sicyonian Treasury. Of the two cuttings in the block drawn uppermost, that on the left is slightly higher than the other; this does not rule out boarding being laid across, for, as we have already seen in the south-west wing of the Propylaia, the cuttings are always liable to minor inaccuracies. The slot ceiling at Aphaia presumably extended the full width across the temple; one imagines that these tympanum slabs came from the west pediment, at which end of the building they are now lying. Whether the peristyle at the east end also had a slot ceiling I do not know.

TEMPLE OF CERES, PAESTUM. There are traces of the sockets for the ceiling beams still to be seen in both pediments, but they are better preserved in the west pediment (Fig. 21 *e*). It is impossible to take detailed measurements, partly because of the poor quality of the stone, which has not weathered well, and partly because it has proved necessary to brick up the sockets. The result is that only the pieces of stone in the intervals between the beams remain visible (Pl. XIII*a*); moreover, I am not too sure just what happens to the beams at the north end of this course (Pl. VI*a*, right). The state of the stonework of this building is such as would make me doubtful of the sockets altogether, were they not so adequately paralleled.

KARDAKI. The side cornice blocks have their inner face cut into a ledge to take the ends of the ceiling beams, as at Sounion and the Theseion. A typical example is shown in Fig. 13 *b* (p. 55). There are no actual cuttings for the beams, but there are a number of dressings, for the stone of this ledge or shelf was carefully smoothed where a beam was to rest on it. These dressings show that the beams were 31–33 cm. wide and 24 cm. apart. This is a fairly wide gap for a slot ceiling (though the slots are still narrower than the beams). The height of the beams we can only guess, but their tops cannot have sat up far above the tops of the cornice blocks. This would give a height of 14·8 cm., which is reasonable in proportion to their known width of 31–33 cm. The span over the side colonnade is about 1·60 m.

DORIC BUILDING, DELPHI. The cornice block shown in Fig. 21*f*, which is of white marble, is lying on the ground near the museum. I have not found out to what building it belongs. The sockets for the ceiling beams are suited to a slot ceiling in that they are closer together than their own width, but they are very narrow. We must not overlook the possibility that they were continued into the course below, giving a series of sockets like those in Pl. XIII*c*.

SOUNION. The arrangement of and evidence for the ceiling of the side peristyle at Sounion is dealt with in Appendix II, pp. 107 ff. Two points deserve notice. One is that the beam and slot proportions as given by the stonework are almost ideal for a slot ceiling, as exemplified in the Propylaia and other well-attested buildings. The other is that this is the only example I know (assuming my restoration to be correct) of a ceiling constructed of wood and stone combined.

The existence of the slot ceiling thus seems to be established beyond all reasonable doubt. Indeed, for that the Propylaia alone would suffice. There is no proof that the slots between the beams were boarded over, but I cannot imagine a ceiling with gaps left open through which it would be possible to look up into the attic; and this is the only alternative. Second, we should note that the boarding laid would provide a very satisfactory floor if there should be occasion for anyone to walk on it.[1] This would make a very suitable type of ceiling to restore over the cella in buildings where the attic was in use.

I have found little evidence for slot ceilings in the stonework of West Greek buildings, but do not doubt that they were extensively used there. It is significant that the South Italian vase painters, when painting one of the little heroa that appear on so many of their pots, almost invariably depict over the pronaos something that looks very like a slot ceiling.[2] Since it is also found at Kardaki and in Attic classical work, its use would seem to be widespread in both space and time.

II

CEILING, ROOF, AND THE
THESEION ARCHITECT

It is a self-evident truth that if one puts the ceiling of the side peristyle high enough it will interfere with the rafters. Although not very common, this did happen, and then a piece of the ceiling had to be sliced off to let the rafters past. We find this difficulty in the Temple of Aphaia, where the bottom of the ceiling is shown by the cornice blocks to have been only 21 cm. below rafter level. Fiechter, in his restoration of it,[1] accordingly has to shave off a corner of the nearest coffer to let the rafter pass. The same difficulty arises in Smith's restoration of the Temple of Zeus at Olympia;[2] Doerpfeld avoided it by restoring a ceiling of planks,[3] which, being thinner than Smith's, did not come near enough to the rafters to interfere. Neither of these is a serious example, for we are dealing with wooden ceilings, the dimensions of which are conjectural. A stone ceiling is much less tractable, and when the same difficulty arises it is not so easily solved.

It arises in all three buildings attributed to the Theseion architect. We have already considered the bottleneck between ceiling and roof that arose at the four corners of the Theseion (pp. 14 ff.); in the other two temples attributed to him the trouble occurs again in more acute form, and at both Sounion and Rhamnous awkward corners of the ceiling had to be shaved off to leave space for the roof (Figs. 22 and 23, pp. 111, 113). The ceiling and the roof were in conflict in two different ways. The side peristyle ceiling was in the way because of the manner in which its beams, parallel in plan to the rafters, converged with them. Of the end peristyle only the two thranoi were in the way, lying across the line of the rafters. The beams of the end ceiling were larger than those down the sides; this meant that they were also higher, and, unless the end ceiling was to be lower than that along the sides, which is most unlikely, then their tops would project further up. Thus it is that when the ceiling and roof come into conflict the part most affected is the thranos. This could only have been cured by moving the thranos either down or inwards, making the ceiling either lower or narrower. The architect apparently considered such cures worse than the disease, and preferred to compromise by keeping both ceiling and roof in position and squeezing in as much of each as he had room for. We have already seen the fruits of this policy in the sloping-topped thranoi of the Theseion. This building apparently convinced the architect of the wisdom of his ideas, for at Sounion we find a relationship of ceiling and roof that is a logical sequel to that of the Theseion.

Our knowledge of the ceilings of the Temple of Poseidon at Sounion stems mainly from the article by Orlandos in *AE* (1917). However, with much of this article I cannot agree. First we may consider a portion of a stone beam to be found among the blocks piled up below the west end of the temple. It is shown in Pl. XV *a* and Fig. 22 *d*. It is plainly a ceiling beam of some sort, but it is much too large for the side colonnade. The question is settled when we observe that the top of the block is not flat but sloped, more or less at roof pitch. This slope, which might possibly be overlooked in a hurried inspection or put down to wear owing to the inaccessible position and badly worn state of the block, and does not show too clearly in my photograph, is plain on close examination and can mean but one thing. This beam is a thranos from the end peristyle, with its top shaved off at an angle to accommodate the rafters. This becomes clear on a comparison of Pl. XV *a* and Pl. III *d*, and Fig. 22 *d* and Fig. 6. Orlandos publishes a drawing (*AE*, 1917, 224, fig. 19) of what he claims to be a beam from the end peristyle and which he says he found on the west slope. It seems plain that this is in fact our thranos, for Orlandos' drawing differs from mine only in that his beam is drawn with a flat top. I am confident that Orlandos did not notice the slope, or, if he did, put it down to weathering,[1] and that we are in fact dealing with the same beam. This, of course, involves no substantial change in the ceiling as he restores it (Orlandos, fig. 21), except that the thranos should be shown with a sloping top.

Of the ceiling beams from the side colonnade several are still to be found. Orlandos has drawn one of these in his fig. 22. My own measurements bear Orlandos out, except that the beams seem to have been rather lower than he says they were. My figures give the height to the top of the crowning moulding as about 15 cm., instead of 23·5 cm., and the width as 37 cm. (this tallies with Orlandos). This gives a beam very shallow indeed in proportion to its width (Fig. 22 *c*), but we shall see the reason for this later. It will be noted that both in the beam shown by Orlandos and that in my own Fig. 22 *e* there is a small piece shaved at an angle off one corner to allow the roof timbers to pass.[2] I found three ceiling beams and each carried this cutting, and in the same place. Probably, therefore, we can assume that it occurred on them all, and that the rafter spacing is the same as that of the ceiling beams, though not coinciding with it. It is on the spacing of these beams over the side peristyle that I disagree most seriously with Orlandos, whose restoration I cannot accept. The spacing is given by the dressings cut to receive the beams where they rested on the inner side of the cornice blocks. Orlandos (p. 225) says: Ὡς πρὸς δὲ τὴν πρὸς ἀλλήλας θέσιν τῶν δοκῶν τῆς περιστάσεως, ταύτην δυνάμεθα κατὰ προσέγγυσιν νὰ εὕρωμεν βοηθούμενοι ὑπὸ τῶν μικρῶν λαξευμάτων τῶν εὑρισκομένων κατὰ τὴν ὀπίσθιον παρειὰν τῶν γείσων τῆς περιστάσεως, ἅτινα εὑρίσκονται εἰς κανονικὰς περίπου ἀπ' ἀλλήλων ἀποστάσεις, καὶ δὴ οὕτως, ὥστε τὸ μεταξὺ τῶν δοκῶν κενὸν νὰ εἶναι κατὰ μέσον ὅρον 0. 41. These dressings are fairly light and could not be called cuttings. They are to be found both on the ledge on which the ceiling beams rested, and on the upright face against which their ends abutted. They are to be found on a great many cornice blocks.[1] They are cut at the same spacing on them all. And that spacing leaves between the beams a gap of not 41 cm. but 24·5 cm.

Typical cornice blocks are shown in Pl. XV *c, e* and in Fig. 22 *a*. In each it can be seen that the dressings are in fact so close together that they are wider than the gaps between them. This is so sharply in conflict with what Orlandos published[2] that I made a special search among all the cornice blocks that I could find. Every single one that had any dressings at all (one was blank, having presumably supported a thranos) had them at this same spacing. These blocks and the spacings on them are shown in Fig. 22 *b*, each diagram representing the back of a cornice block in elevation. In each block in the narrower of the sections marked the stone is left slightly raised, showing that this marks the interval between the beams, represented by the broader divisions on each side. The second block from the top, for some reason, has the dressings only on the ledge and not on the upright face. The actual widths of the dressings vary a little, but on an average they are about 42 cm. wide and 20 cm. apart.

We have already seen that the ceiling beams of the side peristyle were 37 cm. wide. These will fit our dressings very well, leaving the stone dressed for a margin of about 2 cm. on each side. In any case, the rafter cutting on the beams proves conclusively that they came from the side peristyle and rested on these dressings.

We now come to the phenomenon of the beam spacing. This was already close enough on Orlandos' showing, but we are now inexorably faced with a ceiling of marble beams 37 cm. wide and on an average interaxial spacing of 61·8 cm., 24·5 cm. apart. This makes coffers quite impossible. It is perhaps just conceivable that there was a single row of coffers between each beam and its neighbour, but this, I think, cannot be right, for it would be unusual to have but a single row, and very unusual to have them narrower than the beams that they were between. It seems clear that we are dealing with a slot ceiling. A comparison with Table 4 will reveal that the spacing of the beams and their shallowness relative to their width are ideal for a ceiling of this type.[3] Indeed there is nothing, with one important exception, at Sounion to which we cannot readily find a parallel in Table 4. The exception is the fact that the beams are of marble and not of wood, making this the only use known of marble beams with a slot ceiling.

We must now consider what was used to cover the gaps between the beams. It would no doubt be possible to use slabs of marble, thus forming a completely marble ceiling, which would certainly be what one would expect, but it is perhaps not impossible that wood was used. I base this guess on the holes for the dowels to be found on the tops of the ceiling beams. These dowels fastened to the beam whatever was used to cover the slots between them. The holes are to be seen in Fig. 22 *c, e*, Pl. XV *f* and Orlandos, fig. 22. All of them are round.

I know of only one example of the use of round dowels to fix stone to stone; they were employed in one of the Caryatids of the Erechtheion.[1] The only other examples of their use that I know of at all are in the Stoa Poikile,[2] and in the Athenian Treasury at Delphi,[3] where they were used to fix the wooden epikranitis moulding of the cella.

It is thus plain that round dowels were not usually employed in stonework. Their use in the Erechtheion was due to special requirements, for they fulfilled the functions of empolia rather than ordinary dowels.[4] But there was no reason why ordinary elongated dowels should not have been used at Sounion, and the use of round dowels must have had some definite and special purpose. The only explanation that I can offer is that the dowels were used to fix down covers of wood, not stone (cf. the use of round dowels with wood, above). This of course gives us a highly unconventional ceiling—I know of no parallel for a ceiling of stone and wood combined—but I think this a lesser evil than leaving the round dowels unexplained; there must have been some reason for them. The ceiling thus restored is that shown in Fig. 22 f. It should be emphasized that I restore this ceiling only along the side peristyle; across the end peristyle and over the pronaos and opisthodomos arrangements were probably quite different.

As already stated, the interaxial spacing of the beams is 61·8 cm. This figure I arrived at by taking the average of the combined widths of eight dressings and eight intervals, as measured on the cornice blocks shown in Fig. 22 b. From Doerpfeld we learn that the interaxial spacing of the triglyphs was 1·26 m.[5] Since this makes it almost twice the beam spacing, perhaps we are to believe that the ceiling beams too were related to the triglyph spacing, as they apparently were at Rhamnous ($2 \times 61·8 = 123·6$, spacing of two ceiling beams; 126·0, triglyph spacing). If this is correct it is important, for it seems that the rafters, and hence the tile joints, are on the same spacing as the ceiling beams; this confirms Plommer's suspicions[6] that Orlandos' scheme of alternate wide and narrow rows of tiles was an unnecessary elaboration.

We have thus seen how our architect's love of a high ceiling compelled him at Sounion not only to slice off the tops of the thranoi, as in the Theseion, but also to shave off pieces from the side ceiling beams. When we consider our third temple, that of Nemesis at Rhamnous, we see that this trick of his has now involved him in serious trouble. It occurs along the sides of the temple. There have been published three sections of the side cornice. The first is that by Gandy in the Dilettanti publication of the Antiquities of Attica (pl. v). The second is that of Orlandos in BCH, 1924, p. 313. The third is that by Shoe in Profiles of Greek Mouldings, pl. LXXVII. All three of these restorations are impossible, and for the same reason. The ceiling is now set so high that the inevitable has happened and there is no longer any room at all for the rafters to go through to the sloping bed on top of the cornice block.[7] Of the three restorations, the most improbable in appearance is Gandy's, which has actually to shave off a corner of the ceiling to let the tiles past.

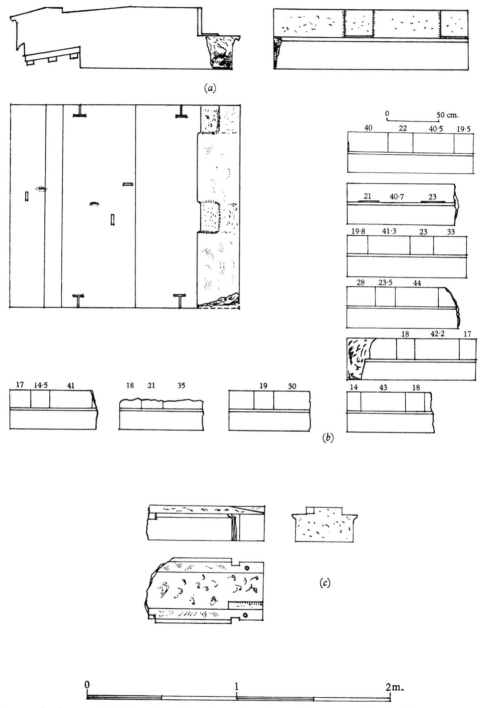

Fig. 22 (and opposite). Temple of Poseidon, Sounion. (a) Cornice block; (b) dressings for ceiling beams on inner faces of cornice blocks; (c) ceiling beam; (d) thranos; (e) relationship of rafters and ceiling beams; (f) restoration of ceiling over side peristyle.

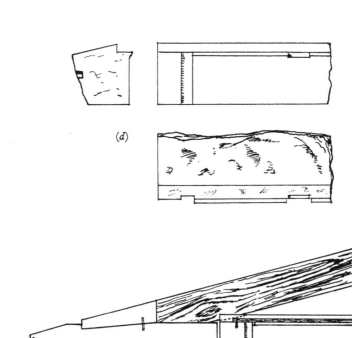

(d)

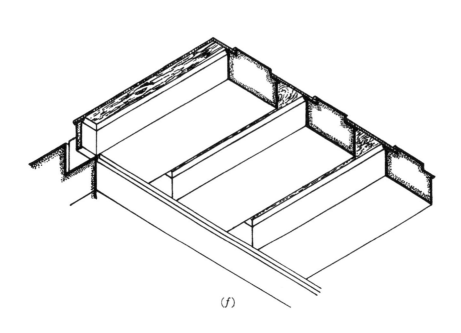

(e)

(f)

III

Of the remaining two, Orlandos omits both ceiling and roof, being concerned only with the cornice. Shoe omits the roof, but, if it were put in, she, like Gandy, would have to shave a corner off her ceiling to let the tiles past. Even with all these expedients, however, there is only room for the tiles themselves—none at all for the rafters. It is plain that if the rafters are to get through, then somehow or other the ceiling must have been lower relative to the roof than anyone has shown it. My own researches show that it was.

I have visited the site three times, remaining a few hours on each occasion. I was therefore unable to devote to the building the detailed study that it so urgently needs. My researches have, however, uncovered certain facts hitherto unnoted and relevant to our purpose. Of the various members with which we are concerned we shall deal first with the cornice block. This is correctly shown by all the restorations, except that none of them mentions that the back of it sometimes contains dressings for the ceiling beams, as at Sounion. Here, however, they are to be found only on the upright face and not on the ledge on which the beams actually rested. They are recessed 2–2·5 cm.[1] One of them is shown in my Fig. 23 *f*.

The wedge block resting on top of the cornice fixes the level of the roof tiles. We may note that since it fixes the level of the top of the tiles the top of the rafters must have come some 4 cm. or so lower;[2] this sets the upper limit of the woodwork.

The ceiling beams were 20·7 cm. high. This I checked, and could find no fragments of any smaller beam.

With the coffers, however, it is a different story. Near the north-east corner of the temple are a large number of small fragments from the coffered ceilings, representing both the coffers themselves and the grids on which they sat. Two fragments of coffer grid are illustrated in Fig. 23 *a, e*; the first of them is also shown in Pl. XVI *a*. The point that comes immediately to the eye is that the end of the block is shaved off in the way with which we have become familiar in the Theseion and at Sounion. This at least demonstrates one thing: there is no glaring error in the published restorations, no magic way out of the difficulty. The ceiling was pressed hard up against the roof, even more closely than usual. It will also be noted that these grids are fairly thin, that shown in Fig. 23 *e* being only 8 cm. thick.[3]

This is a step forward, for it means that rafters are now possible. The end of the grid block, which Gandy and Shoe show as sitting up in a way that effectively blocks all passage, is reduced to much smaller proportions. The ceiling is still not low enough to allow the ends of the rafters to rest on the sloping bed of the cornice block, but at least, for the first time, there is a free space, be it ever so meagre, between tiles and ceiling.

The second discovery that I made was that there were three different types of coffer lid. First there is the fragment marked (*d*). I found three fragments of this type of coffer, which differs from the others in that the coffers and grid are cut out of the same block; one is shown in Pl. XVI *b*. Moreover, they are fairly thick, the one in my drawing being

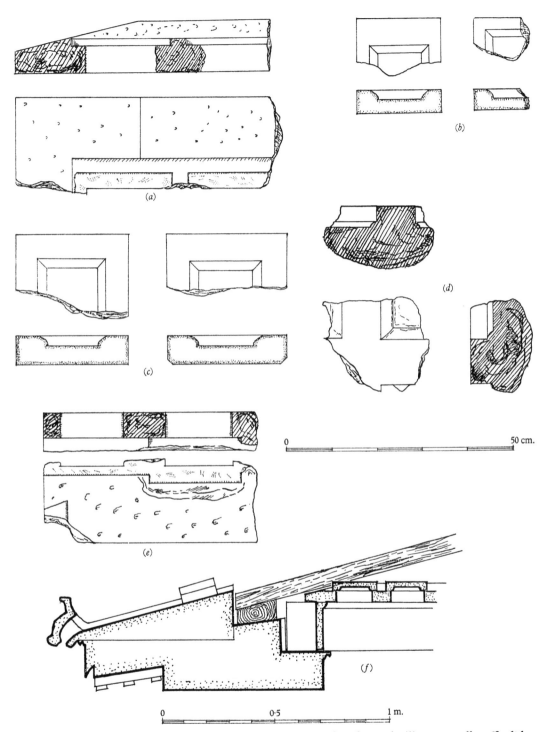

Fig. 23. Temple of Nemesis, Rhamnous. (*a*) Fragment of coffer grid; (*b*) two small coffer lids; (*c*) two coffer lids of the larger type; (*d*) fragment comprising both grid and lid; (*e*) fragment of grid; (*f*) cornice block with dressing for ceiling beam.

preserved to a thickness of 13·5 cm. Not enough is left of any of the blocks to tell us much about the coffers, but they seem to be more or less the same size as those that we shall assign to the end peristyle (see below). The blocks are heavily worn, and the profile of the moulding and such points of detail cannot be considered as certain. My guess is that these fragments come from the ceiling over the pronaos or opisthodomos.

This type of coffer is represented by only three fragments, but of both the others numerous pieces survive. The chief point to be noted is that there are two distinct sets of coffer lids, one being much smaller and thinner than the other. Two blocks of this type, both excellently preserved, are shown in Fig. 23 b. They are respectively 4·8 and 4·2 cm. thick. The inside of the coffer sinking is 10·5 cm. square. It will be seen that the block to the left has an exceptionally wide margin left on one side. This is quite common, and it will be seen that block (e) has been cut to receive such a coffer lid. I would suggest that this may have been a measure adopted to hold the coffer lids firmly in place on top of the grids and arrest any tendency to slip sideways. These wider coffer lids probably came at some regular interval.

The second type of coffer block is represented by the two fragments shown in Fig. 23 c. It will be observed that of all the four fragments shown only the right-hand one of (c) has the bevelled edges restored by Gandy for all the coffers. Fragments with bevelled edges are to be found on the site but are not very numerous. These lids are both wider and thicker than the first type, being 6 cm. thick, with a coffer sinking 11·6 cm. square (measured at the inner edge of the moulding).

It is surely natural to attribute these larger coffers to the ceiling over the end peristyle, where there was more room and the ceiling beams were larger, and the small ones to the side peristyle. We can see that this would agree both with the proportions of the ceiling beams and with the demands of the roof.

We now have all the elements essential to a restoration, and this I have attempted in Fig. 23 f. In it I have used the small coffer lids and a coffer grid 8 cm. thick, as is block (e), tapered off at one end, on the model of block (a). The result of our efforts is that some 9 cm. is now free for the rafters. This is still hardly adequate, and the rafter still fouls the corner of the outermost coffer lid, so that one or the other would have to be cut. Knowing our architect's propensity for removing inconvenient bits of stone, we may make a shrewd guess which it was. I have found no sliced-off coffer lids to support this idea, but the number affected would be proportionately very small. It may well be that even though the span to the cella wall was only 1·05 m. this allowance of 9 cm. was thought insufficient for the rafters; after all, the tiles were of marble. I am inclined to wonder whether a rather thicker rafter may not have been used and some sort of bite cut out of its underside to get it over the coffers. This would mean part of the rafter resting actually on top of the ceiling, and I am loath to believe that the Greeks ever did this, as a general principle at least. This, however, was something of an emergency, and the rafters would be resting on the ceiling beams very near their ends, so that the load would, in effect, be transmitted straight down as usual.

One other difficulty must be mentioned. We have set the level for the bottom of the rafters by building up the various elements of the ceiling. This level is considerably above the sloping rafter bed on the cornice block. There are three possible answers to this. First, a really thick rafter with a bite cut out of it to get it past the ceiling could have its bottom low enough to rest on the bed. Second, there may be some error in our reconstruction of the ceiling. This I think unlikely. The governing factor is the ceiling beams, which are themselves higher than the bed, and would block anything resting on it. We could only assume that the side peristyles were roofed with some tiny beams as yet undiscovered. This seems improbable. The third solution is that adopted in Fig. 23f. Since the bed seems too low, I have raised it by laying a wall-plate to bring it up to rafter level. This is scarcely an ideal solution, but, so far as roof and ceiling are concerned, Rhamnous is scarcely an ideal temple.[1]

Everything springs from the abnormal height of the ceiling. The architect seems to have regarded the woodwork as a minor consideration, and, indeed, having given the ceiling priority it is only by the most strenuous efforts that he was able to find room for the roof timbers at all. His love of the ceiling, it is true, did not prevent him sawing pieces off it where necessary and where it would affect neither its appearance nor its stability, but it was his determination to get the last inch of height for it that caused all the trouble; and it may perhaps be taken as an indication of our architect's abilities that even when ceiling and roof were so acutely in conflict as at Rhamnous, he still contrived by various shifts both to have his cake and eat it.

8-2

III

TECHNICAL TERMS

It is often difficult to establish the ancient technical names for the various parts of the roofing structure. Inscriptions offer a wealth of material, but the scholar will soon find himself bedevilled by the practice, common in the ancient world as in the modern, of not always using the same word to mean the same thing, and a close study is essential before the truth emerges.

The first point to note is that many of these words, being technical terms, do not occur outside building inscriptions; but some are also to be found in literary works, and such references are not a trustworthy guide to the meaning of the word, for when a technical word is used by a writer who is not himself an architect he is liable to give it a meaning rather different from the tradesman speaking of his craft. It is therefore to the technical inscriptions that we must turn our eyes for the truth.

The inscriptions offering the most material are the following:

> *IG*², I, 372–4 (Erechtheion).
> *IG*², II, 463 (Gallery on the Walls).
> *IG*², II, 1668 (Arsenal of Philo).
> *IG*², II, 1672–3 (Work at Eleusis).
> *IG*², IV, 102 (Temple of Asclepios, Epidauros).
> *IG*, XI (2), 144, 156, 161, 287 (Temple accounts, Delos).
> *SIG*, 236–48 (Temple accounts, Delphi).

It will be most convenient to work through the various terms occurring in these inscriptions and referring to the methods and materials used in roof construction, and try to establish the meaning of each.[1]

ὀροφή In literary works this word means little more than 'roof' in its widest and most generic sense, that is, the cover over a house, without distinction between the roof proper and the ceiling (*Odyssey*, XXII, 298; Theophrastos, *HP*, v, iii, 7; *Ar. Clouds*, 173). Herodotus (II, 148) uses the word of the chambers of the labyrinth at Crocodilopolis—ὀροφὴ δὲ πάντων τούτων λιθίνη κατά περ οἱ τοῖχοι. In inscriptions, however, the meaning is rather different.

> *IG*², IV, 102, 42. τὰν ὀροφὰν τὰν ὑπένερθε.
> *IG*², I, 373, 246. κεραμόσαντι ὑπὲρ τῆς ὀροφῆς ἐπὶ τὸ νεό.

These references are plainly to the lower part of the covering over the building, that is, the ceiling. This is confirmed by *IG*, XI, 161, 72, where we read of part of the ὀροφή being whitened by way of decoration, and by other references in the same inscription (for example, l. 45). ὀροφή may therefore be said to be the proper word for 'ceiling'.

We sometimes also find it used in a more ambiguous sense, where it could refer either to the whole roof generically, or at least to the woodwork of it.

IG, XI, 146, 68. κεραμίδων ζεύγη εἰς τὰς ὀροφάς.

SIG, 248, III, 55. ὀροφή occurs in a heavily mutilated passage near a reference to ἐλάτη, a wood used for the roof timbering rather than the ceiling (but in n. 1 to this inscription Dittenberger uses ὀροφή of the cella ceiling).

IG, XI, 156 A, 40. δοκία ὥστε τὰς ὀροφὰς στεγάσαι.

IG², I, 372, 85. τὸς λίθος τὸς ὀροφιαίος τὸς | ἐπὶ τῶν κορῶν ἐπεργάσασθαι ἄνοθεν (this refers to the large stone slabs forming both ceiling and roof of the Caryatid Porch of the Erechtheion).

IG, XI, 287 A, 72. διακεσαμένοις τῆς ὀροφῆς τὰ προσχρηίζοντα καὶ ἀνακεραμώσασιν ΔΗ.

Supp. Epig. Gr. IV, 445, 10. ὀρόφιοι λίθοι.

There is no telling what these are, beyond the fact that they formed some part of the Didymaion at Miletos, but from their being of stone one presumes that we are dealing with the ceiling rather than the roof.

IG², I, 1668, 65. Here ὀροφή is used of the floor of the side galleries of Philo's Arsenal, which, of course, was also the ceiling of the compartment below.

We may also note

ὀροφόω *IG*, XI, 199 A, 104. This is a reference to the covering over parts of a palaistra. As the structures to be so treated include στόαι ἄστεγοι, ὀροφόω presumably means 'to roof' rather than 'to ceil'.

From all this we may deduce that ὀροφή is a loose term which can be used to signify the whole roof and ceiling structure. Properly, however, it refers to the ceiling, and when the speaker is conscious of the distinction between the ceiling and the roof proper it is to the former that ὀροφή refers.

σελίς 'Stone ceiling beam' (L & S).

It is quite plain that σελίς means a beam of the ceiling: the most important references are *IG²*, I, 373, 259 (rebuilding the workshop wall after the beams for the Erechtheion had been carried out); *ibid.* 194 ff., 264; *ibid.* 374, 58; *IG²*, IV, 103, 163 ff.; see also *SIG*, 244 A, 40, note.

None of these references makes it clear whether or not σελίς can also refer to a wooden ceiling beam of the sort that can sometimes be used to support the roof over the cella.

μεσόμνη   (*SIG*, 248, N 9, μεσόδμα).

*IG*², II, 1668, 24, 25; 1673, 35.

This means a wooden crossbeam such as was used to support the ridge beam; unfortunately it is impossible to say if it was used only of structural members, such as in Philo's Arsenal and my restoration of the Temple of Poseidon at Paestum, or could also apply to a ceiling beam fulfilling the same function (it is thus an inversion of the problem of the meaning of σελίς).

ἐποροφία   A term occurring only in *IG*², I, 372, 81, τῆς ἐποροφίας σφηκίσκος καὶ ἱμάντας ἀθέτος; l. 243, ἐς τὴν ἐποροφίαν ἱμάντων ἐργασίας. This plainly means the roofing woodwork (L & S wrongly translate 'roof').

ἐπωροφίς   A term occurring only in the Delian inscriptions. *IG*, XI, 287 A, 62, κατὰ καλλύνασι τὴν κόπρον τῶν περιστερῶν ἀπὸ τῆς ἐπωροφίδος ΔΗΗΙΙΙ (this would seem to have been a major job, for a special payment of three obols is recorded for the conveyance of the κόπρος to the agora).

Inscr. Del. (Dürrbach), 290, 171. Κόνωνι τὴν ἐπωροφίδα ἐγλαβόντι τοῦ νεὼ τῆς Δημῆτρος ἐργάσασθαι καὶ ἐπιθεῖναι.

ὑπωροφία   '(sc. χώρα), the woodwork of a tiled roof' (L & S).

From the etymology of the word one would expect it to mean an under-ceiling, that is, either some sort of canopy hung under the main ceiling or the main ceiling under the roofing woodwork. In fact, it plainly means the roofing woodwork itself.

IG, XI, 161 A, 51. τοῦ νεὼ τοῦ Πωρίνου τὴν ὑπωροφίαν ἐργάσασθαι καὶ ἐπιθεῖναι, παρέχοντας αὐτοὺς αὐτοῖς εἰς τὰ ἔργα πάντα ὅσων ἂν δεῖ πλὴν ξύλων καὶ κεράμου ἠργολάβησαν.

*IG*², IV, 102, 42. . . . Γιμος ἕλετο τᾶς ὑπωρυφίας τὰν ἐργασίαν (this is contrasted a little later with τὰν ὀροφὰν τὰν ὑπένερθε, the ceiling proper). Hiller von Gaertringen (*loc. cit.*) describes it as '"Dachstuhl", cui imponitur ὀροφά', which only makes sense if one translates ὀροφά roof tiles. A little further on, l. 50, the roofing woodwork becomes ἡ ὕλη ἡ ὑπένερθεν.

In spite of the first passage quoted (where it means 'pediment'?) it would thus appear that ἐποροφία is the proper term for roofing woodwork, with ὑπωροφία a variant with the same meaning.

κορυφαῖος   The ridge beam (*IG*², II, 1668, 49). In *IG*², I, 373, 115, it seems to be the apex block of the pediment.

μέλαθρον   In *IG*, XI, 161 A, 105, μέλαθρον, according to Dürrbach, means 'ridge beam', which is also one of the meanings given by L & S.

IG, XI, 199 A, 113. μέλαθρα ὑποθέντι ὑπὸ τὰς δοκοὺς δύο. What μέλαθρον here means must remain uncertain, but the Greek implies that whatever they were they could be put in place from below without disturbing the woodwork on top of them.

παραετίς 'Tile placed on the raking cornice of a pediment' (L & S). Dürrbach, however, on *IG*, XI, 161 A, 55, τοῦ Πωρίνου τὰς παραετίδας (sc. δοκούς) ἆραι καὶ τὰς δοκοθήκας ἐπιτρῆσαι καὶ πάλιν καθαρμόσαι, takes them to be wall-plates, or possibly purlins. This seems to be wrong. αἰετός is the pediment (see *IG²*, I, 372, 188; IV, 102, 89; I, 372, 181, αἰεταῖοι [λίθοι]), and παραετίς should therefore designate something stretching along the pediment.

IG², IV, 102, 100. παραετίδας καὶ ἁγεμόνας καὶ βάθρα τοῖς ἀκρωτηρίοις.

IG², II, 1666 B, 15. Πεντεληικοὺς δύο εἰς τὰς παραετίδας.

These two passages make it plain that L & S translate the word correctly; it means a raking sima tile. If so, however, then the Delos passage becomes very difficult. δοκοθῆκαι looks as if it must mean 'beam sockets' (so L & S. The word is a ἅπαξ λεγόμενον), but then ἐπιτετραίνω becomes a somewhat odd word to use; it should refer to the boring of a hole into a block, not cutting out a large socket, for which some compound of κόπτω would be more suitable. It is remarkable that both τετραίνω and καθαρμόζω appear again in *IG*, VII, 3073, 72. This inscription is a specification for a pavement at Levadia, and one of the operations involved is the removal of some clamps and the deepening of their cuttings: καὶ τρήσας βαθύτερα καθαρμόσει καὶ περιμολυβδοχοήσει δοκίμως. This is an operation much more appositely described by τετραίνω than the cutting out of beam sockets. I am therefore uncertain of the meaning of δοκοθῆκαι, in spite of the plainness of the derivation, beyond the fact that to gain access to them the tiles had to be stripped from the raking cornice and replaced at the conclusion of the work.

σφηκίσκος 'A roof timber, rafter' (L & S). σφηκίσκος is the normal Greek word for a rafter. This is made clear by the Philo inscription, *IG²*, II, 1668, 53, and the word also appears in *IG²*, I, 372, 81, in a context showing it to be one of the secondary timbers (τῆς ἐπορ. ... σφηκίσκος καὶ ἱμάντας ἄθετος). See also under κάλυμμα, below.

The word is also loosely used in Polybius V, 89, 6, to refer to roof timbers in general—Antigonos, we are told, gave the state of Rhodes 10,000 timbers (ξύλα), eight and sixteen cubits long, εἰς σφηκίσκων λόγον.

It is also employed in the Philo inscription (ll. 71 ff.) to designate floor joists (see Doerpfeld, *AM*, 1883, pl. IX).

σφήξ Used as equivalent to σφηκίσκος in *IG*, XI, 146, 65; 156 A (ll. 56, 64, 73, 82). References to τὰ καλύμματα καὶ τοὺς σφῆκας, followed by mention of tiles, make it plain that σφήξ is used as a variant of σφηκίσκος.

Although, however, these inscriptions make certain the identification of σφηκίσκος and σφήξ with the rafter, it is hard to see how it came to bear the meaning. σφηκίσκος should mean literally 'a pointed stick', being derived from σφήξ, a wasp. Indeed Aristophanes, *Plutus*, 307, uses the word to designate a stick used for blinding, for instance, the Cyclops. Why should a rafter be thought of as pointed? My own belief is that it comes from the tapering, pointed end of a rafter as laid on a flat-topped cornice block. It would be interesting to know whether this term was also employed in Western lands, where the sloping-topped block deprived the rafters of their pointed ends, but epigraphical evidence is confined to mainland Greece.

σφήν 'Wedge' (L & S). However, we find in *IG*, XI, 145, 11–12, τοῦ Ἀσκληπείου τὰ πρόπυλα ἐξέδομεν ἐπιστεγάσαι καὶ κεραμῶσαι Πρωτέαι: △ △ △ : ξύλα εἰς δοκία καὶ σφῆνας καὶ καλύμματα △ · εἰς τἆλλα ὅσων ἔδει...*vac*....παρ' Ὀλυμπιάδου: ⊡ : μίλτου, κόλλης: Γ.

It is most unlikely that wood would be bought for the express and sole purpose of cutting it up into wedges, which would surely be an ideal way of using up left-over scraps. Moreover, the σφῆνες are listed along with the other secondary timbers; if wedges were meant, surely they would be included in the τἆλλα ὅσων ἔδει. I therefore believe that σφῆνες here are not wedges but one of the secondary timbers; they are most probably the rafters. I would suggest, then, that σφήν is a Delian variant of σφηκίσκος, and possibly derives its meaning from the wedge-shaped end of a rafter laid on a flat-topped cornice block, as does σφηκίσκος. See also *IG*, XI, 146, 65.

παρασφήνιον 'Side block for wedging' (L & S): it occurs only once with any clue to its sense: in *IG*, XI, 161 A, 98 we learn that it cost 2 drachmae. It also appears in *IG*, XI, 159 A, 38. I should like to think that, with the identification of σφήν with a rafter, παρασφήνιον meant some member lying alongside the rafters, such as the member laid down the inner edge of the raking cornice in my reconstruction of the Temple of Poseidon at Paestum (p. 8); 2 drachmae would be an appropriate price.

δοκίς A vague word. Xenophon (*Cyn.* IX, 15) advocates the concealing of a snare by covering it with δοκίδες of thistle. It also appears in *IG*, XI, 287 A, 24, and in *IG²*, II, 1672, 87, without telling us more than that it is a wooden member used in building and costs 2 drachmae. In the famous *IG²*, II, 463, the specification for the Gallery on the Walls, it is used as meaning a rafter (this inscription is very inaccurate in its use of technical terms, none of which are elsewhere found in the same sense). It seems to be a general word meaning a timber in size midway between a beam and a batten.

ἱμάς Lit., a strap. In an architectural sense it occurs only in the plural. L & S translate 'planks laid on rafters'.

IG², I, 372, 81 (see under σφηκίσκος); *ibid.* 373, 236, χουλοργοῖς ἐς τὲν ἐπορόφιαν ἱμάντας ἀποχσέσασιν μῆκος ἑπταπαλάστος, πλάτος δεκαδακτύλος, τριõν ἑμιοβελίον ἕκαστον: △ △ △ Γ; *ibid.* 248, τὸς σφεκίσκος θέσι καὶ τὸς ἱμάντας.

This makes it quite clear that in these inscriptions, dealing with the Erechtheion, ἱμάντες are either battens or sheathing. That it is the former is shown by the Philo inscription, *IG²*, II, 1668, 55, where it is stipulated that the ἱμάντες be laid on top of the σφηκίσκοι, half a foot wide by two fingers thick, and four fingers apart. This is about the same width as the Erechtheion battens (above).

In *IG*² II, 463, 66 (the Gallery), on the other hand, the ἱμάντες are the sheathing laid on top of the battens. This usage is unparalleled.

ἐπιβλής Not a common word. Neither *IG*, XI, 144 A, 58 nor *IG*², II, 1672, 193 gives any clue to the sense. In the Gallery (*IG*², II, 463, 62) it designates one of the two possible forms of batten. In *IG*², II, 1672, 62 f. (see below under στρωτήρ), from the very low cost—ten ἐπιβλῆτες could be bought for a drachma—we may assume that ἐπιβλῆτες were the light, thin sheathing boards.

στρωτήρ 'A rafter laid upon the bearing beam' (L & S).

This is a word of very wide and general meaning. It designates a member something the same size as a δοκίς, smaller than a δοκός and lacking the flatness of a σανίς (below). Polybius, v, 89, 6, mentions στρωτῆρες seven cubits long.

*IG*², II, 1672, 62–65. δοκοὶ ἠγοράσθησαν παρὰ Φορμίωνος △‖: ἡ δοκὸς △ΓϜϜ: κεφαλαὶ ΗΗϜϜϜϜ: στρωτῆρες ⊞△△△△‖‖‖ παρ' Ἀγάθωνος τοῦ Φιλεταίρου, ὁ στρωτὴρ Ϝ‖‖‖: κεφαλὰ ΗⅣΓ: ἱμάντες παρ' Ἀρχίου Σαμίου △△△△: τιμή △△△△: καλαμίδες παρ' Ἀρτέμιδος ἐκ Πειραιῶς· τιμή ⊞△△: ἐπιβλῆτες παρ' Ἀρχίου Σαμίου ΗΗΗΗ: τιμή △△△△. The distinction in cost between the δοκός, costing seventeen drachmae, and the στρωτήρ, costing one, gives an idea of their relative sizes, as does that between the στρωτήρ and the ἐπιβλής, ten of which could be bought for the price of one στρωτήρ. We may perhaps wonder whether these στρωτῆρες were used as rafters, since that is the only member of the secondary timbers not mentioned in the passage.

In the Gallery inscription (*IG*², I, 463, 62) it is suggested that στρωτῆρες be used as battens, rabbeting them into the rafters. The word also appears in *IG*², IV, 102, 179, 235. It could also be used to designate a flat pantile.

κάλυμμα It is used in the Arsenal inscription (*IG*², II, 1668, 57) to designate the sheathing. It also occurs in *IG*², II, 1682, 27, where its meaning is uncertain, but seems to have something to do with the roof, and in *IG*, XI, 156 A, 73, where, appearing in conjunction with rafters and tiles, it clearly means one of the secondary timbers.

Another common meaning of κάλυμμα was the coffer lid of a ceiling. *IG*², IV, 102, 57 and others makes this plain (the Epidauros inscription, where some of the coffers were decorated with faces); so does *IG*², I, 373, 255, πομφόλυγας τορνεύσαντι ἐς τὰ καλύμματα. *IG*², I, 373, 256, πρίστει ἐς τὰ καλύμματα διαπρίσαντι σφηκίσκον, bears the same meaning. The rafters of the Erechtheion were of large cross-section and could be used to furnish a number of coffer lids by being cut across in the manner of a man slicing a loaf of bread; from the wages recorded as paid out it would appear that the necessary sawing took five days. In *SIG*, 236 inv. 3943, 7, the meaning is uncertain; Dittenberger, relying on the Arsenal inscription, sees in it a reference to sheathing, but, in view of the mention of ὀροφ[ή] in the line above, 'coffer lids' seems a more probable translation.

κάλαμος IG, XI, 144 A, 81. θέντι τὸγ κέραμον Σωσανδρίδηι τοῦ ζεύγους IIC · κάλαμον ἐπιθέντι ἐπὶ τὸν νεὼν τῆς Δημῆτρος Ἀρχικλεῖ μισθὸς ⊢⊢⊢. The tiles here were of terra-cotta, for they cost 1 drachma 2 obols a pair (tiles were normally accounted for in terms of pairs, presumably on the principle that a pantile was by itself useless without the accompanying cover tile), which is much too cheap for marble. It is interesting to see that two men were employed, one to lay the tiles and the other to lay the rushes. We have already noted (pp. 65 ff.) the presence of clay mixed with rushes in the Gallery.

We also find the word καλαμίς, which should mean a bundle of reeds, occurring frequently in inscriptions, especially at Eleusis and particularly in IG², II, 1672; l. 64 has already been quoted (see under στρωτήρ); l. 101 (σχοῖνοι ἐπὶ τὰς ὀροφὰς καὶ καλαμῖδες) defeats me, unless the reference is to some primitive thatched roof, where the σχοῖνοι would be the plaited bands holding the rushes in place; l. 194 tells us that a bundle of rushes cost 4 obols (?). The word also appears in IG, XI, 144 A, 61, possibly referring to kindling for a fire.

ὑποδόκιον. 'The beam on which the rafters rest' (L & S), that is, wall-plate. L & S quote IG², IV, 102, 59 (Epidauros), Πρωταγόρας εἵλετο ἔγκαυσιν τοῦ ὑποδοκίου καὶ κυματίου (here Hiller von Gaertringen says of it 'θρᾶνος quod inter tecti δοκούς et murum templi est'); and also SIG, 247, II, 72 (Delphi), τῶν πλευρίων παρξοᾶς τοῦ ἄνω στίχου τοῦ ὑπὸ τῶι ὑποδοκίωι. On this Dittenberger quotes III, 7, 15, which are repeats of the same phrase, and the Epidauros passage quoted above; he adds: 'τὸ ὑποδόκιον Cavvadias censet significare *statumen tignorum* quae formabant tectum (nostrum "Ortbalken")'. Thus all authorities agree in making ὑποδόκιον a wall-plate holding the feet of the rafters.

This is surely impossible. The Epidauros inscription expressly specifies that the ὑποδόκιον had a painted decoration (ἔγκαυσις). This means that it must have been visible, and thus must have come below ceiling level. A wall-plate in the position described by Cavvadias would be hidden, and any decoration on it pointless.

I would suggest, therefore, that the word refers to some member coming below the ceiling, most probably the broad, raised fillet, generally painted with an anthemion or meander, often found immediately below the hawksbeak of the epikranitis (see RD, 204; *Olympia*, pl. XXIX). Etymologically, the word would mean either the thing that is under the (ceiling) beams, or the beam that is under (the ceiling); no doubt the term dates from the days of wooden construction, when this was a heavy wooden wall-plate to take the weight of the ceiling beams.

θρᾶνος This word can designate a beam in almost any part of the building.

IG², II, 463, 75. καὶ ὅσα κατέρρωγεν τοῦ τείχους ἐνδήσει θράνοις. In the Arsenal inscription (*IG²*, ɪɪ, 1668, 81) it is used of various floor and ceiling beams in the wooden structures occupying each of the side aisles (see Doerpfeld, *AM*, 1883, pl. ɪx).

IG², ɪɪ, 1672, 208. ἱμάντες καὶ θρᾶνοι ἐπὶ τὸ πρόθυρον τοῦ νεωκορίου παρὰ Φίλωνος καὶ εἰς τὸν κέλητα καὶ τὰς κερκίδας ξύλα. An obscure passage. The mention of ἱμάντες leads one to believe that it is something to do with the roofing woodwork, as this word is used in architectural contexts of the secondary timbers and nothing else; but the rest of the passage is quite unintelligible. κερκίς (lit. a shuttle) means either half of a pediment (*IG²*, ɪv, 102, 89, 112), or a long bolt or pin (*IG²*, ɪɪ, 1668, 52). κέλης, normally a racehorse, and hence anything on which one sits astride, is perhaps some sort of prop. I cannot help thinking that the way that the rafters run out from each side of a ridge beam might conceivably remind one of a man on horseback, and if so κέλης should mean the ridge beam itself; but this is completely conjectural.

IG, ɪx, 161 A, 49. τὸν θρᾶνον τοῦ νεὼ τοῦ Ἀπόλλωνος ἐπικόψαντι Νίκωνι μισθὸς δραχμαὶ Γ. Δεινοκράτει τὴν ταινίαν ἐπὶ τὸν θρᾶνον τοῦ νεὼ ἐπιθέντι δραχμαὶ △△△ΓΗΗ. Of this Dürrbach says 'θρᾶνος parietis est supremus lapidum ordo cui ταινία lignea superadditur'. See also *F de Dél*, xɪɪ, 68 ff., esp. 75, n. 1, 'Par θρᾶνος doit être désigné l'élément de bois ou de pierre qui reposait au faîte des murs et où s'asseyaient les abouts des poutres'. This I think is correct. θρᾶνος is the whole of the epikranitis course, ὑποδόκιον a band of decoration on it. The addition of the wooden tainia is peculiar. I would suggest that it was added only on one side of the thranos, the blocks of which carry holes for pairs of large wooden pegs bored into the upper surface of the block and towards that side of it that looked on the peristyle (see *ibid.* 69). Thus the peristyle ceiling would rest on the tainia, the cella ceiling direct on the thranos. This would be a peculiar arrangement, but not impossible.

δοκός A large bearing beam.

IG, xɪ, 161 D, 118. εἰς τὸν ἔμβολον τῶι μελάθρωι δοκὸν ἐκκαιδεκάπηχυν καὶ ἄλλην δοκὸν δεκάπηχυν...ἄλλην δοκὸν ἑνδεκάπηχυν.

IG², ɪɪ, 1673, 35. δοκοὶ εἰς μεσόμνας. δοκός is the term usually applied to large timbers such as would be suitable for use as purlins or ridge beam. As has been seen (above) there exists a diminutive δοκίς which is used of smaller members fit for the secondary timbers.

σανίς A plank. It was a reasonably large timber, for we find in *IG²*, ɪɪ, 1672, 151, 154, 157, σανίδες 10, 16, and 15 ft. long respectively. Some of them were to be used in building a crane. We also find the word used to describe the ταινία to be fitted in the Temple of Apollo on Delos (see above), and also the top of a bench (*SIG*, 244 B, 62). It is thus clear that a σανίς could be of considerable size, but differed from a στρωτήρ or δοκίς in that it was flat, not square, in cross-section. The cross-sections of the σανίδες quoted in *IG²*, ɪɪ, 1672, 151–7 are 10 fingers by 3 fingers, ½ foot by one palm, 3 palms by 6 fingers, and 3 palms by one palm.

κορμός   A tree-trunk (L & S), that is, an undressed log (*IG²*, II, 1672, 191; but see *ibid.* 304, where one of a number of squared logs is described as a κορμός).

ῥυμός   The same (*IG*, XI, 154 A, 18; ῥυμεῖα, pl., in *IG²*, II, 1672, 307).

μοχλός   A small log or stake (*IG²*, II, 1672, 303).

ὀχετός   A door jamb (?) (*IG²*, II, 1672, 305).

ἱστός   Lit., a mast; in *IG²*, II, 1672, 306, a beam used in building a crane.

ξύλα   A general term for timbers of any sort. We hear especially of ξύλα τετράγονα, logs dressed square, in *IG²*, IV, 108, 162; *ibid.* 109, 138; *IG²*, II, 1672, 304.

τόμος   A length of wood cut off a longer beam (*IG*, XI, 165, 49; *ibid.* 161 D, 128). They could on occasion be quite large members. ἀπότομον, *IG*, XI, 287 B, 149; παράτομον, *ibid.* 151.

τρῖμμα   A fragment or cutting from a beam (*IG²*, II, 1672, 303, μοχλῶν τρίνματα ⌐III, ταῦτα εἰσφῆνας [εἰς σφῆνας?] ἀνήλωται.

ἐπίτομα   A trade name for short lengths cut off from a log; trees that were knotty and unsuitable for other use were often so disposed of (Theophrastus, *HP*, v, i, 12).

For the different kinds of wood in use see Theophrastus, *HP*, v, *passim*. The chief varieties mentioned in inscriptions are:

ἐλάτη   Silver fir. This was one of the two woods used in abundance for the Temple of Asclepios at Epidauros, the other being cypress. We are not told specifically where each went, but may guess with reasonable certainty that the silver fir was for the roofing and the cypress for the ceiling (*IG²*, IV, 102, 25). We also find fir used for stage scenery in *IG*, XI, 158 A, 68.

Theophrastus (*HP*, v, i, 5) praises ἐλάτη and πεύκη as κάλλιστα καὶ μέγιστα τῶν ξύλων. ἐλάτη was the usual wood used for the masts and yards of ships; it also had the advantage of holding very firm at glued joints, because of its coarse grain (*HP*, v, vi, 3).

πεύκινος   Pine—*IG²*, I, 342, 70 (Parthenon); it is not known where in the building the timber was employed.

κυπάρισσος   Cypress—*IG²*, IV, 102, 26 (Epidauros), presumably for the ceiling (see above); *IG²*, II, 1672, 191; *IG*, XI, 287 B, 146 (ceiling).

πτελέϊνος   Elm—*IG²*, II, 1672, 151, 154, 157. These were the large σανίδες (q.v.) quoted above. *IG*, XI, 287 B, 146 (ceiling); *IG²*, IV, 102, 45 (doors).

κέδρινος   Cedar—*IG²*, II, 1672, 191 (doors); *IG*, XI, 287 B, 146 (ceiling); *ibid.* 161 D, 92 (ceiling) (?).

ἐλάϊνος Olive—*IG*, XI, 139, 13 (doors); *IG²*, II, 1672, 9 (wedges?).

φοῖνιξ Date palm (cut up εἰς δοκούς)—*IG*, XI, 144 A, 64.

μέλινος Ash—*IG²*, II, 1672, 155—σανίδες for door jambs and lintels.

καρύϊνος Walnut—used for a δοκός, *IG*, XI, 145, 20.

πύξος Boxwood—used for ornaments, *IG*, XI, 287 B, 144; *IG²*, IV, 102, 45, *et al.* For the woods used in the Gordion tombs see *AJA*, 1957, 326; 1958, 148.

In addition we must note:

μονόβολος/δίβολος Of one/two pieces (L & S)—*IG²*, II, 1672, 307. The word is applied to ξύλα of various sorts. Whether this is a reference to composite timbers made of two members fixed together, I cannot say.

ξύλα Μακεδονικά *SIG*, 248, N 8; *IG²*, II, 1672, 66, 304. In spite of Theophrastus, who says that Macedonian wood was the best in the whole of the Aegean (*HP*, V, ii, 1), in this last the consignment of wood in question seems to have been used only for odd jobbing; two of the timbers were used for ἱμάντες. Of course, though it came from Macedonia it may have been poor-quality timber; are we to deduce from this that while silver fir was used for the primary timbers, anything would do for battens and sheathing?

We may also note various operations:

δορόω (See also pp. 65 ff.) This enigmatic verb has plainly a connection with roofing, and also with clay, but further than that it is not really safe to go.

IG², II, 463, 68. καὶ ἐπιβαλὼν κάλαμον λελαμμένον, ὑποβαλὼν λοβὸν ἢ κάλαμον, δορώσει πηλῶι ἠχυρωμένωι πάχος τριδακτύλωι.

Ibid. 73. καὶ ποήσας κανθήλιον...ἐκδορώσει πηλῶι ἠχυρωμένωι....-υτρεχὲς ὕψος τεττάρων στοίχων.

IG², II, 1668, 58. δορώσας κεραμώσει Κορινθίωι κεράμωι.

IG, XI, 156 A, 28. καλαμῖδες δύο ⊦⊦⊦ΙΙΙ· Διονυσίωι δορώσαντι καὶ κα...(*vac.*) (L & S stigmatize this reference as 'dub.').

IG², II, 1682, 30. ...-εψιν καὶ τὴν ἀλιφὴν τῶν ξύλων καὶ τὴν δόρωσιν [καὶ κεράμωσιν π]λὴν κεράμου ἀποδώσει.

ἀλείφω It seems that in small non-monumental buildings the tiles were often treated with pitch to stop up any cracks or bad joins, and we often find ἀλείφω in this sense. *IG*, XII (7), 62, 26. (In *IG*, XI, 144 A, 79, however, it describes some operations performed on the κρηπίς.)

Pitch, indeed, is a commodity often appearing in the building accounts. It was used to coat timbers in almost any position, for example, *IG*, XI, 158 A, 77 (doors); *IG²*, II, 1672, 13 (timbers around a wall); also *ibid.* 171. Likewise *IG²*, IV, 102, 238—Τιμασιθέοι πισσάσιος τῶν κεράμων = = = IIIIC (the building concerned is apparently a treasury). We may also note the remark of the Scholiast to Aristophanes, *Plutus*, l. 1093, πιττῶ δὲ κυρίως ἐστὶ τὸ τὰς νῆας πίσσῃ χρίω, καὶ τὸ τὰ διερρωγότα τῶν ξύλων ἐνοῦν. We may perhaps guess that certain of the roof timbers were sometimes so treated.

κολλάω The word can be used metaphorically (lit. meaning, 'glue') meaning to fix one thing closely to another (Diod. Sic. IV, 76), but its frequent appearance in inscriptions along with items recording the purchase of actual glue makes it plain that the joints in the timbers of Greek buildings were often glued together (though of course they may have been fixed by nails as well).

*IG*², II, 1668, 46 (Arsenal).

It was frequently used for the ceilings: *IG*², IV, 102, 50, κόλλας ἐς τὰς θύρας καὶ τὰν ὕλαν τὰν ὑπένερθεν ⊟⊟⊟⊟⊟⊟⊟ : II apparently refers to the roof timbering (see above under ὑπωροφία), but *IG*², I, 372 E, 8, is plainly the ceiling (cf. also *IG*², I, 373, 207, 216). It is noteworthy that in the Epidauros inscription quoted above the total cost of all the glue used (admittedly an exceptional amount was required because of the very elaborate doors) came to 3200 drachmae, about one fortieth of the total cost of the whole temple; only some 400 drachmae worth was used for the roof timbers.

The best glue was made from ox hides and hooves: *IG*², II, 1672, 161, κόλλα ταυρέα; *IG*², II, 1682, 28, κόλλα ὠμοβόϊος.

περιεγκεντρίζω 'Rabbet' (Caskey, *AJA*, 1910, 306). 'Surround with beams laid in cuttings in rafters' (L & S). The word occurs only in the Gallery inscription (*IG*², II, 463, 62, στεγάσει δοκίσιν καὶ ἐπιβλῆσιν τιθείς, ἐναλλάξ, ἢ στρωτῆρσιν περιενκεντρίσει); ἐγκεντρίζω is well attested in the sense of grafting plants.

Holland, *AJA*, 1950, 351, is unable to fit in the sense 'rabbet' with his restoration of a pavement, and says 'The suggestions of Choisy and Caskey that perienkentrisis is mortising of some sort, seems (*sic*) to me untenable; first because it stretches unduly the basic meaning of the word, and second because it involves too elaborate a form of construction for the comparatively unpretentious work in hand'.

On these two objections we may note first that among the examples quoted in L & S ἐγκεντρίζω only once carries its basic meaning of 'goad', and that in a passage of the Septuagint, while it occurs five times in the sense of 'graft'; second, that Holland's own interpretation involves the upper member of the two to be joined being pressed down on to a spike fixed in the lower, a procedure of which he says 'This is the regular method of dowelling in modern joinery: it is on the whole a rather sophisticated technique'. With this last I agree, and wonder accordingly at his rejection of rabbeting as 'too elaborate'.

πρίζω Saw. *IG*², I, 373, 256 *et al.* The meaning of the word is fixed with complete certainty by Diod. Sic. IV, 76, who attributes the invention to Talos, nephew of Daidalos.

It seems also from the reference in *IG*², I, 313, 129 to a πρίον λιθοπρίστες that saws were also used to cut stone.

λεαίνω Theophr. *HP*, v, iii, 6: 'plane' (Hort, in Loeb edition); 'polish, smooth' (L & S). Another word with much the same meaning is ξέω (see L & S). It occurs notably in the passage in Plato, *Theages* 124 B in which Socrates lists πρίʒω, τρυπάω (drill through), ξέω, and τορνεύω (turn on a lathe) as examples of technical skills.

NOTES

PAGE 3

1 Cf. the differences between the side and end peristyle ceilings in the Parthenon (Penrose, pl. 15), and the variety of ceilings used at Bassae. See also Fig. 22 (Sounion) and pp. 102 f. (Pinakotheke).

PAGE 4

1 No doubt this was common enough for large buildings, but only one other building has sockets for more than two purlins (excluding buildings with Gaggera roofs) actually preserved; this is the Parthenon, which had six (p. 47).

2 The dimensions of the actual sockets (the height being measured from the upper surface of the raking cornice blocks on the higher side of the socket) are 74 cm. wide by 83 cm. high by 56 cm. deep (outer purlin); and 48 cm. wide by 103 cm. high by 56 cm. deep (inner purlin). The ridge beam socket is 67 cm. wide by 103 cm. high (at ridge) by 53 cm. deep. From these heights must be subtracted 29 cm. (the height of the rafters) to find the height of the actual beams. All measurements quoted are from the east pediment.

3 Which were about 24 × 27 cm.

4 It was not at all uncommon for beams to be higher than they were wide (for instance, the Temple of Ceres at Paestum had purlins 37·5 cm. high by 30 cm. wide). The excess of height over width, however, was not usually very great. (See p. 92.)

PAGE 5

1 It is well to bear in mind that this cannot be assumed automatically. Strictly speaking, the cuttings in the pediment of a temple cannot be regarded as sure evidence for the roofing system any further than the first crosswall, generally that over the front of the pronaos, beyond which anything may have happened. Moreover, in the only other temple in which sockets for more than a single pair of purlins are preserved, the Parthenon, G. P. Stevens has recently shown that whether or not the purlins over the cella were in fact laid to correspond with the cuttings in the pediment, the roof construction would have been more satisfactory if they were not. (See p. 47.)

2 A third solution, the building up of the cella wall above epikranitis level in rough uncoursed masonry, suggested as a possibility for the Temple of Apollo on Delos in *F de Dél*, XII, 83, seems improbable.

PAGE 6

1 So P & C, fig. 246. For the somewhat remarkable reconstruction of Adamy, *Architektonik des Altertums*, p. 145, I can see no evidence.

2 For example, the Temple of Asclepios at Agrigento, with headroom of about 1·20 m. (See Serradilfalco, *Antichità della Sicilia*, III, pl. XXXIV. Temple A, Selinus, cannot have had much more.)

PAGE 7

1 So Dinsmoor, p. 111. But, for possible evidence of side galleries (which would involve two stairways), see Choisy, p. 437.

PAGE 8

1 P & C give their interaxial spacing as 67 cm. (P & C, p. 533). I do not understand this at

all, for it is quite incorrect. I measured several sockets with some care, and the dimensions and spacing are as I have given them.

2 Dinsmoor, p. 158 n., refers to Haller's restored tiles at Bassae as 'the largest tiles known' (74·2 × 108 cm.), but presumably he is speaking only of marble tiles.

PAGE 9

1 *Observations on the Hephaisteum*, Hesp. Supp. v.

2 *Three Attic Temples* (B.S.A. 1950).

3 *Op. cit.* fig. 35.

4 *Op. cit.* pp. 73 ff.

PAGE 10

1 My own measurements, not taken under very favourable circumstances, give the distance from the outer face of the south purlin (east end) to the hawksbeak of the side cornice as 3·86 m., which tallies with Koch, pl. 50 (3·865).

2 Distance from centre line of temple to inner face of purlin, 3·025 m. (Dinsmoor, *op. cit.* p. 84 n.), 2·98 (Koch, pl. 41); to inner face of cella wall, 3·12 (Koch, pl. 41). The overhang is well shown by Dinsmoor, *op. cit.* fig. 35. Cf. Plommer, p. 86, for a similar phenomenon at Sounion.

3 *Op. cit.* pp. 37 ff.

4 The widths of the three purlin sockets remaining are: north-west, 39 cm.; south-west, 36·5; south-east, 39·5.

5 See p. 4 and Pl. II a.

6 First, I believe, noted by Dinsmoor (*op. cit.* p. 84 n.).

PAGE 11

1 So narrow a seating is odd in view of the generous sockets provided for other beams in the same building, but it would, I suppose, support the beam safely enough if the other end was held firmly. This would be over the north-west opisthodomos anta, and there

is no evidence what happened there. Of the north-east pediment socket, on the other end of the same beam, only one side is preserved, but it seems to have been recessed the normal distance. So narrow a seating is not, however, unparalleled, for the cuttings in the west pediment of the Temple of Ceres at Paestum show that there both purlins had the incredibly narrow seating of only 9 cm. (See p. 47.)

2 West pediment, 48 cm. wide by 49·2 cm. high; east pediment, 49 cm. wide by 49·7 cm. high (height measured from the ridge).

PAGE 12

1 The measurements given are from the west socket; those from the east socket are slightly different, but the general arrangement is the same.

PAGE 13

1 For evidence on the dovetail joint and its uses see p. 94.

PAGE 14

1 Measured at right angles to the roof pitch, not vertically, which would not give the true thickness of the secondary timbers.

2 Paestum, span over side peristyle, 3·30 m. (K & P); Theseion, span from cella wall to ridge, 3·12 (Koch).

3 This seems the lesser of two evils, for battens cannot be provided without a corresponding weakening of the rafters, whether it be from notches cut for rabbeting or from the reduction in thickness to allow the battens to pass over on top; and the rafters seem thin enough already by Greek standards, as exemplified by Paestum. It should perhaps be emphasized that the point at issue is not whether in fact the Theseion really needed rafters of this thickness, but whether, on the analogy of similar buildings, the Greeks thought it did— a much more reliable guide to the truth.

PAGE 15

1 For a full discussion of the Theseion architect's treatment of the ceiling-roof bottleneck in his temples at Sounion and Rhamnous see Appendix II.

2 These dowels are shown in Koch, *op. cit.* p. 42, as are the clamps. The wedge blocks were first noted by Dinsmoor in *Hesp.* 1940, p. 31; he says: 'Whether the latter (the top surface of the cornice of the Temple of Ares) was intended for a special course provided with rafter sockets, as at Bassae, and in the "Theseum", or merely supported the ends of the rafters directly, remains unknown.' Plommer (pl. VII) restores a wall-plate. The only plan published for the dowels is Koch's.

PAGE 16

1 Shown by Koch, *loc. cit.*, who, however, makes them too regular, and does not show them on the north-west cornice slope, where they exist quite as plainly as on the south-west slope.

PAGE 17

1 The pediments had no facing slabs, the tympanum being built up in coursed masonry, as was usual in less monumental buildings, and the normal rule in Magna Graecia (for example, Concord, Agrigento).

PAGE 18

1 Although neither of these features is peculiar to Gaggera, it is unusual for them to be so pronounced. As in the Theseion, I imagine dovetailed sockets were used simply for security and not with any particular aim of resisting tension (p. 13).

PAGE 20

1 See the section of the cornice, Fig. 8, top left. The tiles are conjectural.

PAGE 21

1 For some account of this problem see pp. 38 ff.

PAGE 24

1 The Christian beam sockets are generally to be found in the lower half of the epikranitis course, but some of those in the cornice blocks seem rather too roughly cut to be ancient; others again seem rather too neat to be Christian. With the exception of that shown in Fig. 7 (which also appears in K & P, fig. 63), none of the sockets has both sides preserved, and it is hard to say how wide they were; but out of the half dozen that I judged reliably ancient on none is the preserved portion of the socket wider than 27·5 cm.

2 These sockets are like that in block *c*, Fig. 7, except that in all only one side is preserved. On most blocks the socket is cut out of one corner of the block; the widths preserved are 13, 27·5, 27, 6·5, 19·5, and 18 cm. The great variation is presumably accounted for by the rest of the socket having been cut in the next block. The last two, however, give the impression, from the way that they have broken, that they were never much wider than 20 cm., so that we seem to be dealing with two different types of socket—one about 17–20 cm. wide (block *c* being a preserved example), and another considerably wider.

3 Whatever the purpose of this socket, it can hardly have been on one of the sides of the pronaos, where K & P (fig. 63) put it. The ceiling beams over the pronaos, if there were any, surely ran across the shorter span, from façade to crosswall.

PAGE 25

1 In their restoration K & P (fig. 156) show only nine beams, having missed out two of the small purlins; how they came to do it I do not know, for the cuttings are quite plain and can easily be counted even from the ground (Pl. V*a*). It is unfortunately difficult to take a photograph showing them clearly (though they can be seen and counted in Pl. IV*a*), but the sockets themselves are perfectly reliable and well-defined, and there

were eight small purlins, not six, as K & P say. Even more incomprehensible is the fact that this error was perpetuated by Marconi (Marconi, *Agrigento*, p. 86).

2 These measurements are all those of the actual stone cuttings, disregarding any allowance to be made for the secondary timbers. The height measurement for the ridge beam is taken from the ridge, and that for the outer purlin from the higher side. All measurements here and elsewhere in the chapter refer to the east end of the building, to which alone I had access.

3 The actual widths of the eight small purlins, reading from north to south along the east pediment and omitting the ridge beam, are: 38, 37, 36, 37, 36, 38, 56 (!), 40 cm. These widths are taken across the tops of the cuttings, which are sometimes slightly wider at the top than the bottom, either because of wear or to let the beam drop into place more easily.

PAGE 26

1 The medieval roof was laid on a number of small timbers approximately repeating the ancient Gaggera roof; they were about 13 cm. square and 13 cm. apart. (Jeffery, *Archaeologia*, 1928, p. 55, thinks they are ancient and give the line of a pitched ceiling over the cella.) The roof, which presumably also formed the ceiling, seems to have covered only the cella, leaving the peristyle open to the air. It was therefore set on a slightly steeper slope than the classical roof, beginning near the ridge and ending on top of the cella walls.

PAGE 29

1 Cf. the small purlins at Gaggera which, in comparable circumstances, were only 20 cm. wide by 23·5 cm. high.

2 The rafters over the side peristyle, according to K & P's fig. 152, were about 15 cm. deep by 33 cm. wide, and these carried more or less the same weight over the same span as the small purlins.

3 I do not assume access to the space over the side peristyle, where there would be no headroom, nor to those portions of the end peristyle that are in line with it. There would, on the other hand, be access to the space over the cella (provided by the stairways), pronaos (this is proved by the door in the crosswall between it and the cella), opisthodomos, and the part of the end peristyle lying between the large outer purlins (proved by the door in the crosswall over the opisthodomos columns).

PAGE 30

1 Cf. Paestum, which, although a much larger temple, had only one. That the two stairways in the Temple of Concord, and in so many other Sicilian temples, were both meant to be used, and not built simply to satisfy the demands of symmetry, seems to be shown by Paestum, where a second stairway, which, apparently, was not needed, was indicated by a dummy entrance, corresponding to the real one opposite, so as to satisfy the law of symmetry; but it was not built and the doorway remained simply the entrance to a cupboard, thereby satisfying the laws of economics and common sense.

2 The moulding is raised above the level of the surrounding stone, which shows that it is original; were it recessed below it one might be tempted, from the rather odd course that it pursues, to believe that it had been cut in Roman times or later.

3 For some consideration of the possible uses of the attic in the Greek temple see pp. 36 ff.

4 If my theory is correct, then our temple is the only example in classical times in which there is absolutely concrete evidence for a sloped ceiling, or, to be more precise, a ceiling and roof combined. The Stoa of Attalos at Athens, however, had such a ceiling over its top floor, as is shown by the fact that the

ceiling beam sockets are cut on the roof pitch, and a similar ceiling has been restored for the Athenian Temple at Delos (*F de Dél*, XII, 186). This was done because of the finding of several carefully smoothed tympanum slabs that were too small to fit the main pediments. They were therefore thought to come from one of the inside crosswalls and, from their finished state, to have been visible from below. This involves a sloping ceiling, but the ceiling itself is quite conjectural. (See p. 40, n. 1.)

PAGE 31

1 Except, of course, the ridge beam, which is *de rigueur*. The cutting for it has presumably disappeared with the apex of the crosswall, which has crumbled away on this side for a distance of some 20–30 cm. down from the ridge. The part missing is just big enough to account for the disappearance of the socket. It is certain that there were no other large beams in the roof, but the possibility that perhaps small sockets other than those for the medieval roof have passed my eye undetected cannot be ruled out. The stone has worn exceptionally badly, and it is often impossible to tell, even at close range, whether a depression is artificial or natural.

2 It may seem peculiar that the attic over the cella, presumably the more important room, should have a less elaborate ceiling than that over the pronaos; but I do not imagine that any of the attics were highly ornamented—just a moderate amount, enough to show that the room was part of the temple proper and not just a loft. Moreover, over the pronaos and end peristyle the architect was influenced by structural as well as aesthetic considerations, remembering the Gaggera roof that so many temples had over these parts.

PAGE 32

1 That is, the flat ceiling of the cella proper, as opposed to the sloping ceiling of the attic.

2 Because it combines these two qualities so admirably I am tempted to wonder whether it may not be the normal type of ceiling to be restored over the cellas of temples provided with stairways.

It might be thought that since the cella walls are preserved *in toto* their top course would give some evidence for the cella and peristyle ceilings, in the shape of beam dressings; but so poor is the quality of the stone that the authorities have had to cover the tops of nearly all the walls first with a liberal layer of cement, then bricks, and finally, surmounting the whole, asbestos sheeting. This makes inspection of the stonework impossible. All features of the woodwork centring around the cella wall—the slot ceiling over the cella, the piers supporting the purlins, and the coffer ceiling over the peristyle—have therefore been restored quite conjecturally.

PAGE 35

1 The evidence for the coffered ceiling is abundant and to be found in building inscriptions. See especially *BCH*, 1905, p. 460, and P & S, pp. 362 ff. For slot ceilings see Appendix I.

2 Treasury of Sicyon, p. 101; Doric Treasury, *F de D*, II, iii, fig. 68; Treasury of Gela, *Olympia*, pl. XLI; the woodwork of this last is highly complex and quite incomprehensible. There are preserved several blocks of the side cornice with cuttings the bottoms of which are horizontal and are presumably for ceiling beams. There are also three blocks of the horizontal cornice carrying similar cuttings 22 cm. wide by 32 cm. high. The cuttings in the side cornice vary greatly in size and shape and it is often impossible to tell whether they belong to ceiling beams or rafters. I do not know how the ceiling was arranged.

3 *Archaeologia*, 1928, pp. 45 ff.

PAGE 36

1 This is well illustrated by the Athenian Treasury, Delphi. This building, in other respects hardly a typical example of Greek roofing, shows well (*RD*, fig. 6) how the heavy crossbeams (*cb*) must carry both the ceiling and the roofing structure, whatever the form of the latter.

2 Pausanias, v, x, 10.

PAGE 37

1 Namely, the Temples of Concord, Hera, Asclepios, and Heracles at Agrigento, Victory at Himera, A at Selinus, and Hera at Foce del Sele (Krauss in Zancani Montuoro, *Foce del Sele*, I, pl. xxxv); and (?) Poseidon at Isthmia (*Hesp.* 1955, p. 113).

2 For further discussion of which see pp. 72 ff.

3 Cf. in modern houses the construction of the loft in which the water tank is placed; it is usually entered through a trapdoor in the ceiling and has no lighting of any kind. For an indication of how infrequently the attic was visited in a temple not equipped with stone stairways (the Heraion at Olympia) see the interesting anecdote in Pausanias, v, xx, 4.

4 For example, Bassae (see Dinsmoor, p. 159).

5 But one possible answer would be that since all the proportions in a large temple are magnified, the single stairway at Paestum could do the work of the two in Concord, Agrigento, for it was wide enough for two people to pass.

6 For a good discussion of the evidence see Choisy, pp. 440 ff.

PAGE 38

1 For an example of the number of offerings in even a small temple (that of Artemis on Delos) see *IG*, XI, 2, 161 B, 1–65, and *BCH*, 1886, p. 461.

2 For example, Poseidon at Paestum, and, probably, most of the Greek mainland temples.

3 *Handbook of Greek Architecture*, p. 12. His point about the steeper pitch of Roman roofs is a good one.

4 Dinsmoor, p. 242. See p. 98, n. 1, for Lawrence's interpretation of Philo.

5 With the exceptions of G Selinus, which was probably not roofed over the cella, and Apollo, Syracuse, for which see p. 42, n. 1. Paestum, with the Temple of Poseidon and the Basilica, also conforms to the Greek rather than the Sicilian model.

PAGE 40

1 There are three exceptions to this rule in my list. One is the Temple of Athena Alea at Tegea, of which I have nothing to say except that it is very advanced in technique in many ways, and late in our period. The Erechtheion does not count because its cella, although wide, is short enough for the ridge beam to span it unaided, so that the question of trusses does not arise. The same argument applies to the Athenian Temple on Delos. I much prefer the French restoration (*F de Dél*, XII, pl. XVIII), which gives the temple a Gaggera roof with coffers set between the purlins, to Dinsmoor, p. 183, who sets them between the rafters. First, the rafters would have to be fairly heavy, and this would place a great strain on the ridge beam, which, of course, could have no intermediate support. Second, rafters of such importance and size would require some sort of socket or cutting in the side cornice blocks, which, however, are perfectly plain (Fig. 18. The point will, however, be better understood from *F de Dél*, *loc. cit.*).

2 Scranton, *AJA*, 1946, p. 93, holds that the purpose of the inside colonnade was purely decorative, not structural, and that this is proved by the fact that in the Theseion it was not in the original design. To this view I partially subscribe. It is plain that many of the smallest buildings with inside colonnades could in fact have been spanned without them.

Both the Theseion and Aphaia are narrower than Sounion, which had no colonnade. But the colonnade, even when not strictly necessary, always made things easier. I suspect also that in time it may have come to have a certain snob value and been used in some of the smaller temples even when not needed, partly as a decoration, and partly to make the temple look more important. This is the sort of thing that might be insisted on over the architect's head and might explain the late addition of one to the Theseion by an architect who did not usually use one.

3 But this probably represents the utmost possible with prop-and-lintel construction. That the Parthenon could in fact have been spanned by prop-and-lintel has been proved recently by Stevens (see p. 47).

4 That is, about 550 (C. Selinus for example).

5 *SIG*, 248 N, 8 records the presence at Delphi of timber from Macedonia which, unless it was transhipped across the Isthmus, must have gone right round by Matapan: either way would mean a long enough voyage to obviate any improbability in the import of timber from Sicilian forests. This may have been done because the quality of the local timber at Delphi was very poor (Theophrastus, *HP*, v, ii, 1) and may not be a reliable guide to normal practice, but it shows that wood could be transported over a long distance if there was good reason for it.

PAGE 41

1 There are foundations for a large base in the middle, but I am assured by Professor Emil Kunze that it had nothing to do with the roof, which was a free span from wall to wall. Of the roofing he continues, 'es bleibt kaum etwas anderes übrig, als für die Überbrückung der Spannung eine kühne und ungewöhnliche Konstruktion anzunehmen'.

2 The large number is due to one or more rebuilds of the Treasury.

3 Being in fact smaller than the ridge beam that it is supporting, cf. the crossbeams of the Sicyonian Treasury (about 50×25 cm. high, for a span of 5·21 m.); cf. also the rafters over the side peristyle of the Temple of Poseidon at Paestum, which were about 27×24 cm. and carried one row of tiles over a span of 3·20 m., while the crossbeams of the Treasury would have to carry the whole roof over a span of 9·68 m.

4 Wide spans are of course a feature of Sicilian temples. We often hear talk of the narrow Sicilian cella, but their temples are so large that, though narrower in relation to the whole temple, the cella is in fact fully as wide as its counterpart on the mainland (see Table 1 and cf. for example Apollo Corinth and C Selinus).

PAGE 42

1 This, incidentally, could well explain the presence of an interior colonnade in Apollo Syracuse, which is otherwise unparalleled in Sicily: it is there because the temple was built before the Carthaginians and their trusses arrived on the scene. Dinsmoor (p. 75) dates it about 565, Robertson (*Handbook*, p. 69) to the 'very early years of the sixth century B.C.', while to Cultrera it is 'notoriamente arcaico' (*Rivista del R. Inst. d'Arch. e Storia dell'Arte*, 1942, p. 54; see also *MA*, 1952, p. 815). For some account of the relations between Carthage and Sicily see Frézouls, *BCH*, 1955. The influence of the Carthaginians on the Sicilian Greeks' building is something of which we know much less than we ought to, but in the present state of general ignorance of Punic architecture this can scarcely be avoided. There are a number of Carthaginian house models in the museum at Palermo which have the appearance of little heroa, more or less on the Greek pattern, but these do not help us here, except as an indication that the two styles of architecture were not so diverse as

to rule out the possibility of mutual influence. For the models see Gabrici, *MA*, 1929, 41 ff. It seems plain, however, that the powerful Carthaginian colonies could not have existed so long and so close to the Greek cities without influencing them to some extent—cf. the Carthaginian habit of striking coinage modelled on that of the Greek states (Head, *Historia Nummorum*, pp. 161 f.). In general, it seems to have been the Carthaginians who copied the Greeks rather than vice versa, but we must not forget the skill in woodwork of their shipwrights.

Another very early, if non-Greek, building with a remarkably wide span is the eighth-century megaron of the West Phrygian House on the city mound at Gordion, with a clear span of 9·73 m. For this Rodney Young suggests a truss on the strength of the great distance to be bridged and the known skill in mortising of the local carpenters (see *AJA*, 1957, 322, and *Türk Arkeoloji Dergisi*, VII, i (1957), p. 7).

The widest span ever covered by a wooden roof is, so far as I know, the 150 ft. clear span of the Tabernacle at Salt Lake City, built in 1863 by William Faulkener, a local railroad engineer skilled in the construction of trestle bridges. It is an arched roof with ribs 10 ft. thick built up in a lattice formation, and uses no nails or bolts, all the joins being made by wooden pegs and cowhide thongs.

Another discovery of Young's at Gordion, the wooden tomb (*AJA*, 1958, pp. 148 f.), is worth notice as an example of what the ancients could do with wood. Its roof was built of juniper beams about 35 cm. square, over a span of 6·20 m., with one supporting crossbeam; this structure successfully supported the weight of a tumulus about 50 m. high.

2 Cf. the fact that the Sicilians (and the western Greeks generally) hardly ever used the clamps and dowels that are an integral part of mainland construction (K & P, p. 226).

There are many differences between western and mainland building techniques.

3 We may also note the light-hearted readiness with which Athens voted an expedition against so powerful a state as Syracuse in 416, suggesting that the average Athenian had little idea of Sicilian affairs.

PAGE 44

1 See Doerpfeld, *AM*, 1883, pl. VIII.

PAGE 45

1 Although, according to D. S. Robertson, *Handbook*, p. 183 n., W. Marstrand, in a work inaccessible to me, disputes its existence in the Arsenal of Philo. On it see also Jeppesen, *Paradeigmata* (Aarhus, 1958), pp. 81 ff.

It is of course possible that the ridge beam was omitted over the cella in buildings employing the truss; a number of trusses set fairly close together would permit a continuous decking of large battens to be laid on top of them, eliminating ridge beam and rafters. This, however, would be a somewhat revolutionary and advanced structure, and I doubt whether a people as backward architecturally as the Sicilians could have evolved it (unless truss construction had already reached this stage under the Carthaginians). In view of the almost complete absence of evidence for cella roofs it is hard to say just how trusses were employed, but I would suggest that they were set at intervals of 5 m. or so, and supported either a ridge beam and rafters of the usual sort, or a Gaggera roof. This is of course pure guesswork, but the presence of such a roof over the cella of the Megaron of Demeter supports the latter alternative.

2 See Plommer, p. 86, for a discrepancy in the spacing of the purlins at Sounion. Other buildings where the purlins were aligned on the cella walls (that is, so laid that all the purlin was over the wall, but not necessarily centred over it) are the Temples of Ceres

and Poseidon at Paestum and Concord at Agrigento.

3 Excluding Gaggera roofs.

4 These sockets do not always give the true size of the timbers, for two reasons: (a) we may have to deduct a certain amount from the height to allow for the secondary timbers; and (b) I am advised by a practising modern architect that it would be necessary to leave a certain space free between the beam and the stone so as to allow the former to swell in wet weather; he suggests that with a beam 30 cm. square about 0·5–1 cm. be left free all round. As this is so small a percentage it has been neglected in all my drawings and the beam drawn up to the limits of the socket.

PAGE 47

1 This cutting can only be seen for what it is from very close quarters. Examination from the ground or from photographs is useless.

PAGE 48

1 This system was described to me personally by Mr Stevens. That illustrated in the article quoted puts a slightly greater strain on the wood, but is more in accord with traditional Greek practice.

2 The rafters over the central aisle of the Parthenon, so often quoted as an almost impossibly wide span, were shorter, being about 5·45 m. long. There are, of course, many buildings with a longer span from ridge to eaves than the Pinakotheke, but in them the span is usually broken by purlins, which are impossible in the Pinakotheke because of the hip roof. Its rafter span is, however, beaten by the side peristyle of G Selinus, which one presumes was roofed, and if so by plain rafters from cella wall to side cornice.

PAGE 49

1 And can be seen in the two crosswalls preserved there (Pl. IV, a, b).

2 F de D, II, p. 48.

3 IG², II, 1668, 46.

PAGE 50

1 Except in the Temple of Artemis on Corcyra, where, according to Rodenwaldt, Korkyra, I, fig. 45, the sockets were half in the tympanum blocks and half in the raking cornice.

PAGE 52

1 That in the block shown in Pl. VII b is 1·3 cm. wider and 0·5 cm. deeper. It seems to be widening towards the mouth, but this is not preserved and the difference in the part of the socket remaining is too small to be conclusive.

2 For further discussion of this see p. 74.

PAGE 53

1 In fact, of course, the sockets certainly contained purlins and the purlins certainly were tilted. The point at issue is, how many of these purlins were there? Were there only two, aligned on the cella wall and peculiar only in being tilted, or were there enough of them to form a Gaggera roof, being peculiar only by their size?

PAGE 54

1 Korkyra, I, figs. 43, 45.

PAGE 56

1 Paolo Orsi, Templum Apollinis Alaei, p. 57, fig. 28.

2 For instance, Gaggera itself.

3 The Athenian Treasury and Ceres at Paestum.

4 The Temple of Concord, where the Gaggera roof helped to ornament the attic; and the Metroon (if that is where the block belongs; I must admit I wish I could see grounds for attributing it to one of the Treasuries; it has two cuttings for H clamps, the heads of which are shorter than those of the clamps in the preserved courses of the Metroon (6·3 cm. as against 8–9 cm.), which may possibly be an indication); and Hera at Agrigento,

which is doubtful anyway, and may have had not a Gaggera roof but normal tilted purlins. It is also possible to draw quite different conclusions from a study of Tables 2 and 3, and see in the Gaggera roof a form peculiar to Sicily, irrespective of date, but its presence at Aphaia and Zeus Olympia argues against this.

5 But the Treasury may have been modelled on the cella, which would not be affected by a Gaggera roof.

PAGE 58

1 See, for example, Concord, Agrigento, Fig. 9, top.

2 See Andren, *Architectural Terracottas from Etrusco-Italian Temples* (Skrifter Utgivna av Svenska Institutet i Rom, 1940), pp. xxv–xxxiv.

PAGE 59

1 *Op. cit.* pl. 79. The projection too is a non-Greek feature, for in Greek buildings the ridge beam remains invisible from outside.

2 Statues have been found with the base cut in a V-shape so as to fit on to the ridge.

3 With the exception of a single model, illustrated by Andren, *op. cit.* p. xxix, which has a pair of small tilted purlins. For Vitruvius' temple see Vitruvius, IV, p. 7.

4 Of it Professor Caputo, Superintendent of the Museum, says: 'Il coperchio 5496 proviene dalle antiche collezioni Granducali e ne sono ignote la provenienza e le condizioni del trovamento. Così isolato, esso e difficilimente databile; probabilmente appartiene ad un periodo tardo (IV–III sec. a. C.).' On top of the lid the tiling immediately above the supposed truss is different from the rest, and seems to run at right angles to it, but I cannot see how this either affects or throws light on the argument.

PAGE 60

1 Noted by Dinsmoor, p. 159.

PAGE 61

1 Best published by Caskey, *AJA*, 1901, who, in addition to his own restoration, publishes also the interpretations of Choisy and Muller. Holland, in *AJA*, 1950, has made a determined and skilful attack on the whole idea that this is a specification for a roof at all, interpreting it instead as referring to a pavement to be laid along the top of the walls. For this view he makes out quite a plausible case, but only at the expense of certain improbabilities. For one thing, the whole structure seems needlessly elaborate; nor do I like the look of the long boards sloping up to hold the top of the γεῖσον which might perhaps break under the strain of people continually treading on them.

2 IG^2, II, 1668. It is published by Doerpfeld in *AM*, 1883.

PAGE 62

1 Curtius and others: *Olympia: Die Ergebnisse der vom Deutschen Reich veranstalteten Ausgrabungen.*

2 *AM*, 1883. It is noteworthy that in this work Doerpfeld unconventionally laid the sheathing parallel to the battens, covering the gaps between them, instead of at right angles to them, as was more usually restored. His idea was that the resulting 'serrated' effect would give the clay a better grip on the roof. He thought better of this when he came to restore Olympia.

3 *Aegina*, pls. 39, 40.

4 P & S, p. 369 n.

5 I do not know on what he based this belief, but presume that he had noticed the batten cuttings shown in Pl. XI*a*.

6 So P & S, pp. 368–9; Dinsmoor, p. 159; Caskey, *AJA*, 1910, 307; Stevens, *Hesp.* 1950, 177. Marquand, *Handbook of Greek Architecture*, p. 11, prescribes rafters, battens, and sheathing as standard construction, but says nothing of clay. P & C, p. 387, who believe that the use of clay had its origin in

an archaic terrace-roof (which may be right), hold that the clay layer is to be found only in earlier buildings, where it is a throw-back to the terrace-roof; in later buildings the tiles were laid on the wood and the clay added only in 'travaux qui exigeaient une exécution rapide'. This last proviso was presumably added to explain its presence in the Arsenal and the Gallery, and I must confess that I find it unconvincing.

7 So Dugas, *Le Sanctuaire d'Aléa Athéna à Tegée*, pl. xiv. Likewise Plommer, pl. 8 (Sounion), following Orlandos, *A. Delt.* 1915, 19, fig. 13. In none of these works is there any mention in the text. Dinsmoor also omits the battens at Bassae, because of the correspondence between tile and rafter spacing (Dinsmoor, p. 159).

PAGE 64

1 Only found in Italy.

2 A very common form in Greece. A further legacy from the past is the fact that in this form of construction the rows of tiles often end in an antefix decorated with a palmette.

PAGE 65

1 According to the tile standard in the Agora at Athens, as published by Stevens in *Hesp.* 1950, p. 177. This agrees with the tile standard found at Assos (F. H. Bacon, *Investigations at Assos*, p. 71). Stevens declares (*loc. cit.* p. 178) that Laconian tiles had to be bedded in clay to prevent them splitting down the centre, and with the very thin ones that he quotes (2 cm. thick) he is quite likely to be right. His eminently logical and reasonable remark that 'It is obvious that a bed of clay required continuous boarding beneath it' sounds as though it must be right, but runs sadly counter to the anything but continuous boarding described in the Gallery inscription (see p. 67 and Fig. 15).

PAGE 66

1 The only scholar to restore clay under the cover tiles in any building seems to be Rodenwaldt, who does it in the Temple of Artemis on Corcyra (*Korkyra*, I, fig. 45).

PAGE 67

1 Though I have seen this done in modern work, very rarely.

PAGE 68

1 Which would have to be at least 8 cm. thick (the Gallery inscription says 'three fingers', but the tiles at Paestum were much larger and heavier).

2 *Olympische Forschungen*, p. 88.

PAGE 69

1 καλύμματα, it is true, are mentioned, and in the Arsenal inscription this seems to mean sheathing; but in the Erechtheion it apparently designates the coffer lids. See Appendix III, p. 121.

PAGE 71

1 *Aegina*, pls. 39, 40.

2 Cockerell, pl. 10.

PAGE 72

1 *Korkyra*, I, fig. 45.

2 Dugas, *op. cit.* pls. xiv, xlviii; Rodenwaldt, *Korkyra*, I, figs. 27–8; K & P, figs. 85 (D Selinus), 92 (A Selinus); Dyggve, pl. xv (from the number of fragments published it looks safe enough); also conjecturally restored in *F de Dél*, xii, pl. xviii (Temple of the Athenians) and pl. x (?) (Temple of Apollo); and by Orlandos, *A. Delt.* 1915, p. 103 (Temple of Apollo on Mount Ptoos).

3 That this was in fact done is proved by the Temple of Nemesis at Rhamnous, where I found fragments of both wedge-shaped and ordinary flat tiles.

4 Dinsmoor, p. 151 n. In the absence of a more detailed reference I have not been able

to check many of these; but we may notice *Olympia*, p. 17 (Temple of Zeus); Cockerell, pl. VII (Bassae); Dyggve, Poulsen and Rhomaios, *Heroon von Kalydon*, p. 342, fig. 48 H; Orsi, *MA*, 1916, p. 767, fig. 43 (Caulonia).

PAGE 73

1 I have not myself seen the Bassae tile and must rely on the publications. One would like to believe that these pierced tiles illuminated the frieze, but this would mean the provision of a sloped ceiling, as in the Athenian Temple on Delos (this seems preferable to the only other alternative, that of a normal flat ceiling with holes left open in it to let through light from the attic).

2 Which, of course, does not necessarily mean that it could actually have been built. For the hypaethral temple see also R. de Launay, *Rev. Arch.* 1912, I, 365, and II, 143.

PAGE 76

1 Kawerau, *Antike Denkmaeler*, II, pl. 49, and Dyggve, pls. XII, XVI, XXI.

2 The two slabs from Kalydon were restored horizontally by Dyggve, as was that from Thermon by Kawerau.

3 'The entire hypothesis appears to be without foundation'—Dinsmoor, p. 82 n. But see my pp. 89 ff.

4 Cf. for example the Athenian Treasury at Delphi.

5 *MA*, 1933–5, pp. 142 ff.

PAGE 77

1 Gabrici, *op. cit.* pp. 147–8, 215, 219, pl. IV.

2 Which is that shown in Pl. IX*b*.

3 For the relevance of this to the battens/clay problem see p. 72.

4 Gabrici, *op. cit.* pl. XIII, K & P, fig. 78. For the Chinese roof see above, p. 89.

PAGE 82

1 P. 20.

2 It seems certain that the large cuttings in the cornice of the Sicyonian Treasury must be for the ceiling beams and not connected with the roof in any way, in spite of the fact that they are cut at a slightly upward tilt. For Doerpfeld's restoration see Fig. 17. The block from Delphi is also shown in Fig. 21; it is to be found in the dump near the museum.

3 Plommer, p. 111.

PAGE 83

1 *A. Delt.* 1915, p. 25.

2 See my p. 15, n. 2.

3 These sockets were of the dovetailed type, for which see p. 94.

PAGE 84

1 Dugas, *Le Sanctuaire d'Aléa Athéna à Tegée*, pl. XLIV.

PAGE 85

1 See p. 40, n. 1; for Cyrene, Pl. XI*c*.

PAGE 86

1 The block illustrated is from the south-west wing; it also appears in Pl. XIV*b*. The cornice on the Pinakotheke had no sockets for the rafters. On the east hexastyle the cornice blocks are perfectly flat with an eaves block laid on top, after the manner of the Parthenon.

2 The date seems safely fixed for around 480; see K & P, p. 52, and Dinsmoor, p. 109 n. Shoe, *Western Greek Mouldings*, pp. 5, 41, finds its mouldings of a very early form, but accepts the conventional dating. She also sees in it an echo of the temples of Agrigento, which is interesting in view of their common peculiarities in cornice structure (Shoe, p. 25).

PAGE 87

1 P. 68.

2 Doerpfeld (*Olympia*, pl. XLI) is slightly in error here, showing the top of the block at a

slightly shallower angle than the rafter, which, of course, must be at roof pitch.

3 Cockerell, pl. X; *Aegina*, pl. 40.

PAGE 88

1 Durm, *Handbuch der Architektur*, p. 188.

PAGE 89

1 Dinsmoor, p. 82 n. For a general account of Chinese roofs see Dyggve, pp. 307 ff.

2 Krauss, 'Die Giebelfront des sog. Cerestempel im Paestum', *RM*, 1931, 1–8. His conclusions are quoted by Dinsmoor, p. 96.

3 Dyggve, pl. XXIII, figs. 177, 179–81.

4 *MA*, 1933–5, pl. XVI.

PAGE 90

1 Sestieri, *Not. Scav.* 1952, 107.

PAGE 93

1 These are the usual proportions and spacing of rafters in Etruscan tombs. Only in the Hypogaeum of the Volumnii at Perugia do they get as close together as rafters 42 cm. wide and 25 cm. apart (see *RM*, 1942, p. 133).

2 50 cm. is about the average size of those parts of the rafter cuttings that are left, but all the blocks are like the one illustrated in that we never get both sides of the same rafter cutting preserved. They may therefore have been wider than 50 cm. Incredible as it may seem, there is actually one block with a preserved portion of cutting 66 cm. wide. This will plainly give us a rafter rather wider than the tile, which would be not only unparalleled but also unbelievable. Yet there is no other solution that I can see, and I have, with the greatest reluctance, come to the conclusion that the rafters of the south-west wing were either great slabs of woodwork all cut out of one piece, or rafters of normal size laid in close-packed batches. Either way there can be no relation to the tile spacing (not that this would be any objection with the rafters forming a practically continuous

deck). This roof both puzzles and disturbs me.

PAGE 94

1 49·5 cm. wide at the mouth and 51·5 cm. at the back. These measurements are taken at the bottom of the socket; it is rather wider at the top (mouth, 51·7 cm.), for the socket is bell-mouthed as well as dovetailed, after the fashion of Gaggera (Fig. 7), in which, however, the tapers are much more pronounced. A certain number of the rafter sockets in the Treasury of Gela at Olympia also seem to be dovetailed, but it is so slight that it could be put down to natural weathering.

2 This applies only to sockets cut in the stone to take the ends of beams, and not to joins between wood and wood in carpentry proper, of which we know, and can know, very little (see below).

3 Erechtheion, north porth (ridge beam); Temple of Concord, purlins; Megaron of Demeter, purlins. Again, some of the cuttings in the Treasury of Gela (doubtful).

PAGE 95

1 Not counting the round dowels quoted in Appendix II, p. 109; here we are speaking only of the dowelling of major structural members. It is noteworthy that in the Temple of Apollo on Delos wooden pegs seem to have been used to fasten parts of the peristyle ceiling, which was of wood, to the cella wall (*F de Dél*, XII, 69). In the Stoa of Attalos at Athens the Pergamene capitals of the upper inside order of columns bear the holes of medium-sized square dowels (5 cm. square, 6 cm. deep) that fastened down the architraves, which were of wood; it also seems probable that the upper front architrave-frieze backers were of wood, and if so were dowelled to the stone (for the above information I am indebted to Professor Homer A. Thompson, Director of the Agora Excavations). This

is interesting, but of course the Stoa is somewhat outside our period.

2 This view, of course, reflects the theory that the colonnade was the first part of a Greek temple to be built. This theory is in the main based on three buildings, the Temple of Thoricos, the Temple of Aphaia, and the Temple of Segesta.

Of the three, Thoricos is very doubtful indeed. It has never been properly excavated, and it is not even certain that the building was a temple at all, for it is not orientated east-west and has a doorway or gateway through the middle of one of the long sides (see Stais, *Praktika*, 1893, p. 16 and pl. II). Moreover, according to the Dilettanti publication, ch. IX, capitals were found lying in the centre of the temple, so it may well have had some sort of structure inside.

At Aegina the case rests on the presence in the north side of three columns built up of drums, while all the other peristyle columns are monolithic. These three, it is argued, were left until the last to give a gap through which the materials for the building of the cella could be brought through the completed colonnade. This sounds convincing enough, and I accept it.

At Segesta it has been doubted whether a cella ever existed at all, and one could wish for an excavation, however cursory, in the cella area. As it is, a search through the old publications is instructive. Serradifalco, I, p. 114 and pl. IV, Hittorf, p. 39 and pl. III, and K & P, p. 133 and pl. XIX, all record the presence in the centre of the temple of ashlar blocks apparently from the cella. Moreover, the number diminishes steadily: Serradifalco, writing in 1834, saw five sets of stonework, each consisting of several blocks; Hittorf saw two sets in 1870; when K & P arrived in 1899 there were left only two loose blocks, only one of which they marked on their plan. It is this gradual looting that has brought matters to such a pass that Dinsmoor,

p. 112, can now say 'The cella apparently was never built'.

The evidence for the building of the colonnade first thus seems, with the exception of Aphaia, somewhat uncertain. Moreover, there are at least two pointers in the opposite direction.

One is afforded by Temple G, Selinus. Here the columns may be divided into three chronological groups by the style of the capital; and the capitals of the internal colonnade are of the earlier style (K & P, p. 122). Indeed, some of the peristyle columns may never have been erected at all, for the drums for them are still to be seen half-cut in the quarries of Cave di Cusa.

Moreover, it would appear from the building inscriptions of the fourth-century Temple of Apollo at Delphi that there the cella and the colonnade reached entablature level at about the same time. Certainly they record the placing of the corner cornice blocks (*SIG*, 246, H 2, 51) and metopes (*ibid*. II, 69) along with work on the frieze of pronaos and opisthodomos (*ibid*. III, 35).

3 This is assuming that they were not in fact made and later covered over in unskilful attempts at restoration and preservation. K & P, p. 135, remark, not without justice, 'Die Giebel sind im Inneren vielfach ausgeflickt, ebenso das Schräggeison'.

4 Hittorf shows a row of three such blocks as the normal type of entablature (Hittorf and Zanth, *Recueil des Monuments de Ségeste et de Sélinonte*, pl. 44).

PAGE 96

1 Another interesting discrepancy is to be noted in the north porch of the Erechtheion. A row of sockets cut in the cornice gives the rafter spacing accurately. There is also a light well, the walls of which came up almost to tile level and caused some interference with the rafters. The second rafter from the south on the east slope of this roof abutted against

the top of the light well, continuing on to the ridge on the far side of it. The first rafter, on the other hand, was so aligned that half of its width overlapped the well, so that on reaching it it must have been reduced to half of its width; half would be stopped against the wall of the well, and the other half continued along the side until it was past the well, when it resumed its normal thickness, and went on to the ridge. This treatment, though unexpected, would not weaken the rafter very much, as it would be supported by the well while alongside it. See P & S, p. 95, fig. 63.

PAGE 97

1 See Appendix III, p. 125.

PAGE 98

1 Which surely militates against the reconstruction of A. W. Lawrence (*Greek Architecture*, p. 260), who sets this block upright, thus necessitating a pin about five feet long. We may also note that, by the provision of pins and suitable jointing where the crossbeams and rafters meet the purlins, he has turned the roofing system into a series of trusses. This is a serious point, and I wish he had discussed it in his text.

2 Young, *AJA*, 1957, 325, and pl. 91, fig. 16.

PAGE 101

1 See, for example, P & S, pp. 362 f.

2 For example, Doerpfeld restored a ceiling of plain boards over the side peristyles of the Temple of Zeus at Olympia (*Olympia*, pl. XI). So did Fiechter for the Propylaia at the sanctuary of Aphaia (*Aegina*, pl. 58). Audiat restored a ceiling of some very thin woodwork (he does not give a detailed drawing) in the Athenian Treasury at Delphi, but I do not accept it (*RD*, pp. 204 f. and fig. 3).

3 Its existence has sometimes been recognized in individual buildings, but no one has attempted to collect or correlate all the examples of its use.

We may also here mention the other two types of wooden ceiling known. One is known to us from the Temple of Poseidon at Paestum and consists of very broad and relatively shallow planks laid across the peristyle at wide intervals, which were presumably boarded over. The Basilica at Paestum, on the other hand, carries holes for very small, square ceiling beams, centred over the columns and cut in the top of the architrave. This would give an unusual ceiling composed of narrow beams set far apart, and with expanses of plain boarding in between. It is generally held, however, that these holes were cut by mistake since they would place the ceiling below the architrave crowning moulding, and also have no answering holes in the architrave over the pronaos columns, which would be needed to hold up the other end of the ceiling beams. Moreover, one of them has been blocked up. I am not altogether happy about this explanation. It means that the ceiling beam sockets must have been cut before the architrave crowning member was in place, or even thought of, and it seems to have been the Greek practice to leave the cutting of the sockets till the stonework was complete. I have sometimes wondered whether these sockets could represent an unfulfilled later scheme for lowering the ceiling rather than a mistake during the original construction. As has been noted, the beams would form a rather odd ceiling, but they would make an eminently sensible floor (they approximate quite closely to the proportions and spacing of the floor beams cut in the lower architrave of the inside colonnade at Aphaia), and it is, I suppose, possible that someone once wanted to extend the cella attic over the side peristyles. This would mean lowering the peristyle ceiling to give the necessary space (the peristyle ceiling was actually rather high, for in one place the frieze backers are preserved to their full height, but bear no epikranitis moulding). Whatever the plan, it was evidently never completed.

PAGE 102

1 *Olympia*, pl. XXIX.
2 See Pl. XId. Doerpfeld (*loc. cit.*) erroneously shows them as square. It should also be noted that Doerpfeld did not board over the slots between the beams, but left them open.
3 See Pl. XIIIb, and Doerpfeld, *AM*, 1885, pl. V, p. 6.
4 Dinsmoor's restoration (Dinsmoor, p. 200) seems to go wrong here. He also restores a slot ceiling across the east hexastyle. This may be right, but I would have thought coffers more likely.
5 The actual widths of beam sockets and slots, in order east to west, are: south wall (in cm.), 23·5, 14, 53·5, 10·8, 51, 14, 48, 14·5, —, —, 48, 14, 47·5, 14·5, 14·5, 47, 15, 48·7, 13·5, 48, 14, —; north wall, 23, 10, 49, 7·3, 55·3, 11, 53, 12·5, 49·5, 17, 49, 13·5, 49·5, 14 (sockets marked with a dash '—' either are incomplete or I was unable to measure them).
6 The cella, or Pinakotheke proper, had a ceiling of very much heavier beams, on an average 38 cm. broad by 41 cm. high, set on a spacing leaving 60 cm. free between them—ideal proportions for a coffered ceiling.

PAGE 104

1 *Aegina*, pl. 46.
2 Fiechter (*Aegina, loc. cit.*) publishes complete sockets giving a beam width of 45·5 cm.

PAGE 105

1 This was not, of course, the only reason for its use, for of the buildings listed in Table 4 the only two where it seems possible that there was any access to the roof space are Aphaia and Ceres at Paestum, and even these are highly doubtful. It may perhaps be

significant that all the evidence for wooden coffered ceilings comes from Greece, as opposed to Magna Graecia, where access to the attic was less common than in the West.
2 See, for example, *CVA* Lecce II, pl. 33, 3, and Trendall, *Vasi Dipinti del Vaticano*, pl. IV a.

PAGE 106

1 *Aegina*, pl. 40.
2 Smith, *Mem. Amer. Acad. Rome*, 1924, pl. LXI.
3 *Olympia*, pl. XI.

PAGE 107

1 Which I am almost sure it is not. The beam is badly worn, but parts of the sloping top still bear their original pock-mark dressing.
2 Its existence is briefly noted by Orlandos in his text (p. 226).

PAGE 108

1 The few exceptions left plain presumably supported a thranos.
2 Though admittedly he does not expressly say that the dressings are 41 cm. apart, limiting himself to remarking that that was the interval between the beams.
3 The fact that these beams were not, after all, for a coffered ceiling may explain the almost unparalleled use of a cyma reversa for their crowning moulding (Shoe, *Greek Mouldings*, p. 80).

PAGE 109

1 P & S, pl. XXVIII. They were in common use in fastening together pieces of sculpture, and this may have influenced their choice for the Caryatids.
2 *Hesp.* 1950, 328.
3 *F de D*, II, 2, 47–8. It should be noted that these were not iron dowels in the proper sense of the word, but lead pins.
4 The point at issue is that an ordinary dowel has to be set in the edge of the uppermost of the two blocks that it is uniting, to enable the lead to be poured around it *in situ* (for

the technique of dowelling in classical times see the very interesting article of Livadefs, 'The Structural Iron of the Parthenon', in the *Journal of the Iron and Steel Institute*, Feb. 1956). It was not until Hellenistic times that the use of pour channels came in, enabling the dowel to be set in from the edge of the block. Thus in classical times dowels of the ordinary kind could not have been used in the Caryatid, for it would have meant their being visible in the side of the statue.

5 *AM*, 1884, p. 335. Plommer, p. 79, quotes Doerpfeld's figure. Blouet, 1·25; Stais, 1·26–7.

6 Plommer, p. 86.

7 This difficulty was first noted by Plommer, p. 101 n.; it also looks as if the same thing happened in the Temple of Ares (McAllister, *Hesp.* 1959, figs. 13, 21, 23). Exactly the same difficulty arose in the Temple at Priene: see Wilberg, *AM*, 1914, p. 72, and Von Gerkan, *AM*, 1918, p. 165, esp. fig. 2.

PAGE 112

1 They are about 39 cm. wide and 51 cm. apart, edge to edge. These measurements cannot of course be used as they stand to give the ceiling beam spacing, and there are too few dressings for us to work out a reliable average. I see no reason to query Gandy's spacing of 94·5 cm.

2 Battens or similar extravagances are of course quite out of the question at Rhamnous.

3 It is also noteworthy as preserving part of the socket for a dovetail clamp. Several such cuttings are to be found in the remains of the coffer grids; from their shallowness it looks as if they were filled with poured lead alone, without any iron clamp. H clamps were used throughout the rest of the building, except the orthostates. This parallels the Theseion, which is built with H clamps but changes over to the zeta type for the ceiling coffer grids.

PAGE 115

1 It might be just possible that, Rhamnous being such a small temple, there was some kind of a Gaggera roof over the cella and side peristyles. This would make it possible to dispense with rafters altogether, but I rather fancy that it would create more problems than it would solve. It would be particularly interesting to know what the thranos was like at Rhamnous. We know that the end peristyle ceiling beams were rather larger than those along the flanks, so that, as at Sounion and the Theseion, the thranos would sit up in the way of the timbers even more than the side ceiling, which, one might almost say, is impossible. Perhaps it was moved inwards a little so as to clear the rafters. If so, this would make the end peristyle ceiling rather narrower, and one effect of this could well be that the ceiling beam spacing would observe the unit instead of slightly exceeding it, as it does in Gandy's restoration: 94 cm. instead of 98 cm. If the beams were set on a 94 cm. spacing (as on the side peristyle) instead of 98 cm., this would allow each thranos to be moved inwards 16 cm., increasing the height above it by about 5 cm. See Gandy, pl. VIII; Plommer, p. 104.

PAGE 116

1 Of special value to this study is the recent work by Orlandos, Τὰ Ὑλικὰ Δομῆς τῶν Ἀρχαίων Ἑλλήνων (Athens, 1955), especially pp. 18 ff. and 36 ff.

BIBLIOGRAPHY

It is not easy to give a bibliography to a subject on which so little has been written, but, in addition to the various references to particular buildings to be found in my text, the following may be of general interest:

CASKEY, 'The Roofed Gallery on the Walls of Athens', *AJA*, 1910, p. 298.

CHOISY, *Histoire de l'architecture*, vol. I, pp. 279 ff. and pp. 440 ff.

DOERPFELD, 'Das Skeuothek des Philon', *AM*, 1883, p. 147.

DURM, *Handbuch der Architektur*, pp. 186 ff.

JEPPESEN, *Paradeigmata* (Jutland Archaeological Society Publications, vol. IV, Aarhus, 1958), pp. 81 ff.

KOLDEWEY and PUCHSTEIN, *Die griechischen Tempel in Unteritalien und Sicilien*, p. 211.

MARQUAND, *Handbook of Greek Architecture*, pp. 2 ff.

ORLANDOS, Τὰ Ὑλικὰ Δομῆς τῶν Ἀρχαίων Ἑλλήνων, vol. I (Athens, 1955), esp. pp. 18 ff., 36 ff.

PATON and STEVENS, *The Erechtheum*, esp. pp. 368 ff.

PERROT and CHIPIEZ, *Histoire de l'art dans l'antiquité*, vol. VII, pp. 531 ff.

INDEX

The more important references are printed in heavy type

Greek words are listed in the alphabetical position that they would occupy if transliterated into English letters

146

THE PLATES

PLATE I

(*a*) Temple of Poseidon, Paestum: side cornice, from the south-east.

(*b*) Temple of Poseidon, Paestum: inside colonnade.

PLATE II

(*a*) Temple of Poseidon, Paestum: west pediment.

(*b*) Temple of Poseidon, Paestum: cella, from the west.

PLATE III

(a) The west pediment of the Theseion, showing sockets for primary timbers.

(b) Theseion: socket for ridge beam.

(c) Theseion: thranos, north-west corner.

(d) Theseion: thranos, south-east corner.

PLATE IV

(*a*) Temple of Concord, Agrigento, as seen from the east.

(*b*) Temple of Concord, Agrigento: pronaos crosswall.

PLATE V

(a) Temple of Concord, Agrigento: inner face of east pediment, seen from below.

(b) Temple of Concord, Agrigento: south end of pronaos crosswall.

(c) Megaron of Demeter: tympanum block from west wall (?), shown as block a in Fig. 7.

PLATE VI

(a) Temple of Ceres, Paestum: west pediment, showing
sockets for primary timbers and ceiling beams.

(b) Sounion: tympanum backer, showing purlin socket.

(c) Sounion: the two blocks forming the ridge beam socket
(top and bottom centre).

PLATE VII

(a) Doric Temple, Cori: inside face of pediment.

(b) Aphaia: inner face of raking cornice block, showing purlin cutting.

(c) Aphaia: raking cornice block.

PLATE VIII

(a) Modern building at Selinunte (Selinus).

(b) E Selinus: block from crosswall (?).

(c) Lid of Etruscan stone cinerary chest, seen from one end: no. 5496, Archaeological Museum, Florence.

(d) Metroon at Olympia: tympanum block.

PLATE IX

(*a*) Nemea: side cornice block.

(*b*) Delphi: Doric cornice block in red sandstone.

(*c*) The roof of the British School at Athens.

(*d*) Pompeii: modern roof in the Casa dei Vetii.

PLATE X

(a) Treasury of Gela, Olympia: side cornice blocks,
as seen from inside the building.

(b) Treasury of Gela, Olympia: side cornice blocks.

PLATE XI

(*a*) Pinakotheke: groove cut to receive roof in east wall, showing recesses cut to receive battens.

(*c*) Delphi: cornice block of the Treasury of Cyrene, showing rafter cutting.

(*d*) Sicyonian Treasury, Olympia: side cornice block.

(*b*) Pompeii: modern roof over part of the Casa dei Vetii.

(*e*) Treasury of Gela, Olympia: side cornice block.

PLATE XII

(*a*) Paestum: underground shrine.

(*b*) Paestum: underground shrine.

PLATE XIII

(*a*) Temple of Ceres, Paestum: ceiling beam sockets in west pediment.

(*b*) Propylaia, south-west wing: ceiling beam cuttings.

(*c*) Pompeii: colonnade along the forum.

(*d*) Epipoli: pierced tile.

PLATE XIV

(*a*) Segesta: east pediment.

(*b*) Propylaia: cornice block from
south-west wing.

(*c*) Stratos: top of Ionic cornice block.

PLATE XV

(a) Sounion: thranos.

(b) E Selinus: wedge block
from side cornice.

(c) Sounion: side cornice block.

(d) Sounion: side cornice block (upside down).

(e) Sounion: side cornice block.

(f) Sounion: ceiling beam
from side peristyle.

PLATE XVI

(*a*) Rhamnous: fragment of
ceiling coffer grid.

(*b*) Rhamnous: fragment of
(pronaos?) ceiling.

(*c*) Rhamnous: fragments of large and (nearest to camera) small coffer lids.
Right: large and small coffer blocks set upside down to show difference in thickness.